Spotlight on Young Children

Observation and Assessment

Holly Bohart and Rossella Procopio, editors

National Association for the Education of Young Children
Washington, DC

National Association for the
Education of Young Children
1313 L Street NW, Suite 500
Washington, DC 20005-4101
202-232-8777 • 800-424-2460
NAEYC.org

NAEYC Books

Senior Director, Content Strategy
and Development
Susan Friedman

Editor in Chief
Kathy Charner

Senior Creative Design Manager
Audra Meckstroth

Senior Editor
Holly Bohart

Publishing Manager
Francine Markowitz

Associate Editor
Rossella Procopio

Through its publications program,
the National Association for the
Education of Young Children
(NAEYC) provides a forum for
discussion of major issues and
ideas in the early childhood
field, with the hope of provoking
thought and promoting
professional growth. The views
expressed or implied in this book
are not necessarily those of the
Association.

The following selections were previously published in the specified
issues of *Young Children*: J. Jones, "Framing the Assessment
Discussion," January 2004; H. Seitz, "The Power of Documentation in
the Early Childhood Classroom," March 2008; M. Caspe, A. Seltzer,
J.L. Kennedy, M. Cappio, and C. DeLorenzo, "Engaging Families in the
Child Assessment Process," July 2013; J. Elicker and M.B. McMullen,
"Appropriate and Meaningful Assessment in Family-Centered
Programs," July 2013; E.V. Laski, "Portfolio Picks: An Approach for
Developing Children's Metacognition," July 2013; T. Wright and B.
Murray, "Developing a Performance-Based Report Card," May 2015;
and E. Regenstein, M.C. Connors, R. Romero-Jurado, and J. Weiner,
"Effective Kindergarten Readiness Assessments: Influencing Policy,
Informing Instruction, and Creating Joyful Classrooms," March 2018.

The following selections were previously published in the specified
issues of *Teaching Young Children*: J. Pack, "Learning Stories,"
December 2015/January 2016; and A. Eckhoff and S.M. Linder, "Using
Observation to Build STEAM Experiences," August/September 2017.

The "Supporting Children with Delays or Disabilities" sidebars on
pages 28, 42, and 74 are by Monica Lesperance.

Permissions

Portions of "Facing the Challenge of Accurately Assessing Dual
Language Learners' Learning and Achievement," by Linda M. Espinosa
on pages 58–67, are adapted, with the author's permission, from the
following:

L.M. Espinosa, "Perspectives on Assessment of DLLs' Development
& Learning, Prek-Third Grade," commissioned paper presented at the
National Research Summit on the Early Care and Education of Dual
Language Learners (Washington, DC, 2014).

L.M. Espinosa & V. Gutiérrez-Clellen, "Assessment of Young Dual
Language Learners in Preschool," in *California's Best Practices for Dual
Language Learners: Research Overview Papers*, eds. F. Ong &
J. McLean (Sacramento, CA: Governor's State Advisory Council on
Early Learning and Care, 2013), 172–208.

Cover Photo Credits

Copyright © Getty Images: all

Library of Congress Control Number: 2018935987

ISBN: 978-1-938113-34-5

Item 2842

Contents

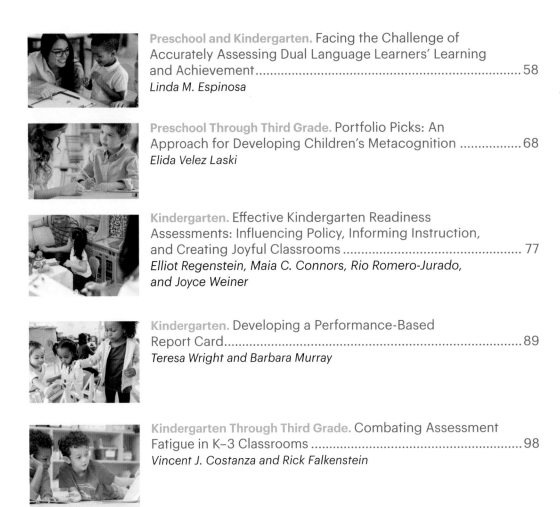

Introduction

Shannon Riley-Ayers

Several years ago I visited a kindergarten classroom to mentor a teacher on collecting anecdotes and using those anecdotal records as evidence for children's learning and guidance for planning instruction. Working in the math center with Tiffany, an outgoing young kindergartner, I took out my pen and sticky notes and began recording what she was doing.

Immediately Tiffany asked, "What you writing?" I responded that I was writing down what we were doing together.

"You writing something bad about me?" she said.

I answered quickly, "Definitely not. Would you like me to read what I'm writing to you?"

After I read the anecdote to Tiffany, she relaxed and we worked side by side, with me taking notes and sharing them with her along the way.

The following month I returned to Tiffany's classroom to continue supporting the teacher. Tiffany and I, old friends now, shared a hello as I went to work with the teacher and a group of other children. From across the room Tiffany called to me, "Ms. Shannon! I'm doing something good here. You want to write it down?"

Just as I explained my note-taking process to a wary Tiffany, I've done a lot of explaining to teachers, leaders, and policy makers about effective assessment and defining what it looks like in early childhood. And like Tiffany, educators who understand the process and benefits of collecting information on what children know and can do and then using it to guide instruction and promote children's learning—known as *formative assessment*—embrace it.

Formative assessment is a critical piece of a balanced, comprehensive system of assessment for young children that also includes screening, diagnostic tests, and summative assessments (Riley-Ayers 2014). It occurs over time in varied situations and through natural observation and documentation in authentic contexts, like a teacher writing an anecdotal note about a toddler's discovery of different textures while playing with materials in the art area. Formative assessment often involves work samples or products that children generate or create, like a second grader's poem or a preschooler's painting. It is the most appropriate assessment approach for young children because their development is highly complex, dynamic, and often erratic and uneven (Ackerman & Coley 2012), which makes it difficult to capture learning through one-time assessments that provide only a snapshot of a child in a particular moment. Formative assessment can also shed light on those areas of a child's development—such as social and emotional skills and approaches to learning—that other types of assessment often overlook.

What Formative Assessment Isn't—and Is

Formative assessment provides a process for teachers to gather evidence of children's learning and to make instructional decisions. This type of assessment

> Is not standardized, with a one-size-fits-all model. While it is systematic in that it has a fixed plan and structure, it is individualized, flexible to meet the context, and comprehensive. It considers every aspect of a child's learning and development, not just her academic understandings.

> Is not simply the act of collecting information. It is the collection *and use* of the information to inform instruction, plan interactions that scaffold learning, and communicate children's progress to them, their families, and others.

> Is not punitive. It acknowledges individual learning and a range of development trajectories. It values where children are, what they bring to the learning environment, and where they are ready to go next. It is a strengths-based approach that allows successes to be celebrated and used as building blocks for further development and learning.

> Does not take time away from learning and exploring. Rather, it *embraces* play and exploration; since children demonstrate stronger skills through play (Hirsh-Pasek et al. 2009) and play enhances their learning (Ilgaz et al. 2018), teachers get a more complete picture of a child's knowledge and abilities with formative assessment. Teaching is assessment, and assessment is teaching—they are not separate acts.

> Is not intended to be used to make high-stakes decisions about a child or teacher. While results from formative assessments can provide insight into such decision making as part of a comprehensive approach, the data they provide are not intended to be used alone.

Educators as Participant-Observers

To reap the full benefits of formative assessment for both teaching and learning, teachers act as participant-observers and engage in an iterative process of five steps (Riley-Ayers et al. 2012):

1. **Observe** and **investigate** children as individuals. This can quickly become a seamless part of instruction and interaction (as demonstrated with Tiffany in the opening vignette). "Learning Stories" on pages 45–49, along with several other articles in this volume, demonstrates the power and usefulness of observing young children during their day-to-day routines.

2. **Document** and **reflect** on what you see and hear children doing. "The Power of Documentation in the Early Childhood Classroom" on pages 50–57 discusses a variety of formats through which evidence of children's learning can be collected and displayed.

3. **Analyze** and **evaluate** the collected data in relation to learning goals or a trajectory of learning. See "Portfolio Picks: An Approach for Developing Children's Metacognition" on pages 68–76 to examine the important role children can play in analyzing evidence of their own learning.

4. **Hypothesize** and **plan.** Consider what strengths, interests, and needs the children are demonstrating and the implications for instruction (Which child might need a different approach? Who needs a bit more of a challenge?). This is the critical step—using the data to support the child's learning through intentional instruction and interactions. Many of the articles in this collection discuss the use of data to plan instruction. This is the core of assessment in early childhood.

5. **Guide** and **instruct.** Finally, target the needs of each child and scaffold his learning to the next level. This leads back to the first step of observing and investigating children's actions and reactions to the instruction, and the cycle begins again.

Assessment is a key component of effective teaching with students of any age. The articles in this collection demonstrate the important role of careful observation and formative assessment in early childhood teaching, learning, and development.

Shannon Riley-Ayers, PhD, is a senior program officer at the Nicholson Foundation. She is a former kindergarten teacher and is the lead author of the *Early Learning Scale* (ELS), a formative assessment tool for preschool and kindergarten children. Her work focuses on improving outcomes for young children.

Jacqueline Jones begins with a broad discussion overviewing the process of the appropriate assessment of young children in her article, "Reframing the Assessment Discussion." In it, she argues for increased assessment literacy and poses a set of questions that are fundamental to understanding the purposes, types, and uses of assessment.

Keeping up with new and updated terminology related to standards and assessment is an essential component of being an effective early childhood educator. **Elena Bodrova** and **Deborah J. Leong** provide clear, timely definitions for an extensive list of key words in "Common Assessment Terms and How to Use Them: A Glossary for Early Childhood Educators."

Appropriate assessment of infants' and toddlers' development is a key process in high-quality, family-focused programs for children under age 3. In "Appropriate and Meaningful Assessment in Family-Centered Programs," **James Elicker** and **Mary Benson McMullen** explain how reflective observation, documentation of individual children's daily activities and growth, regular conversations with families and colleagues, and organized systems for recordkeeping, goal setting, and monitoring development are all parts of an effective assessment system.

Families play an integral role in children's learning and development and are key partners with early childhood educators in the child assessment process. In "Engaging Families in the Child Assessment Process," **Margaret Caspe, Andrew Seltzer, Joy Lorenzo Kennedy, Moira Cappio,** and **Cristian DeLorenzo** explore how collaborative assessment allows families and educators to share responsibility for children's learning and discuss practices for engaging families in the assessment process.

In "Using Observation to Build STEAM Experiences," **Angela Eckhoff** and **Sandra M. Linder** discuss how classroom observations can be used to support children's learning during science, technology, engineering, art, and mathematics (STEAM) investigations. They present ideas and tips for teachers to create meaningful, STEAM-rich classroom experiences that are grounded in children's interests and understandings.

"Learning Stories" describes a simple but engaging documentation technique where teachers write short stories about what they observe children doing during play. **Judi Pack** reflects on how this approach can be used to better understand young children, plan more intentional learning experiences, and show children—and their families—that you value and respect what they do.

"The Power of Documentation in the Early Childhood Classroom," by **Hilary Seitz,** reviews what documentation is, the formats it can take, and how teachers of young children can use it to effectively make children's learning visible to families, administrators, and others in the early childhood community.

In "Facing the Challenge of Accurately Assessing Dual Language Learners' Learning and Achievement," Linda M. Espinosa outlines some of the challenges that arise when assessing the development and learning of children who are acquiring two or more languages. The author gives an overview of what is needed to overcome these challenges, including knowledge of how individual and contextual factors affect children's development, understanding the uses and limitation of assessments, and team collaboration.

Elida Velez Laski delves into how the portfolio assessment method can be used to guide children in self-assessment and development of metacognition. In her article, "Portfolio Picks: An Approach for Developing Children's Metacognition," she draws on her past experience as a kindergarten teacher to provide concrete strategies that help children take initiative in their learning and recognize both their progress and opportunities for growth.

Kindergarten readiness assessments can be an extremely valuable tool for teachers to understand students' learning and development, improve their own practice, and even bring more joy to the classroom. In "Effective Kindergarten Readiness Assessments," Elliot Regenstein, Maia C. Connors, Rio Romero-Jurado, and Joyce Weiner explain that implementing these assessments can also help administrators and families understand and support great kindergarten practice and provide guidance to policy makers to inform early learning investments.

Teresa Wright and Barbara Murray share how a Florida school district used the 12 principles of child development outlined in NAEYC's position statement on developmentally appropriate practice to rethink and reshape a more effective progress report to communicate children's learning. In their article, "Developing a Performance-Based Report Card," they share the process of developing the new report card as well as examples of the performance codes and report card indicators.

In "Combating Assessment Fatigue in K–3 Classrooms," Vincent J. Costanza and Rick Falkenstein discuss an issue experienced by many educators working in kindergarten through third grade. They argue that making the assessment landscape look rational to teachers, children, and families requires clear strategies to bring coherence to assessment approaches, a stronger relationship between curriculum and assessment, and an updated assessment research base.

References

Ackerman, D.J., & R.J. Coley. 2012. *State Pre-K Assessment Policies: Issues and Status.* Policy information report. Princeton, NJ: Educational Testing Service. www.ets.org/Media/Research/pdf/PIC-PRE-K.pdf.

Hirsh-Pasek, K., R.M. Golinkoff, L.E. Berk, & D.G. Singer. 2009. *A Mandate for Playful Learning in Preschool: Presenting the Evidence.* Oxford: Oxford University Press.

Ilgaz, H., B. Hassinger-Das, K. Hirsh-Pasek, & R.M. Golinkoff. 2018. "Making the Case for Playful Learning." In *International Handbook of Early Childhood Education,* eds. M. Fleer & B. van Oers, 1245–63. Springer International Handbooks of Education. Dordrecht, The Netherlands: Springer.

Riley-Ayers, S. 2014. *Formative Assessment: Guidance for Early Childhood Policymakers.* Policy report of the Center on Enhancing Early Learning Outcomes (CEELO). New Brunswick, NJ: CEELO. http://ceelo.org/wp-content/uploads/2014/04/ceelo_policy_report_formative_assessment.pdf.

Riley-Ayers, S., J. Stevenson-Garcia, E. Frede, & K. Brenneman. 2012. *Early Learning Scale.* Carson, CA: Lakeshore Learning Materials.

Photographs: pp. 1, 3, © Getty Images

Reframing the Assessment Discussion

Jacqueline Jones

I n the years since the publication of "Framing the Assessment Discussion" (Jones 2004), there has been a significant focus on early childhood education. The field has experienced increases in state-funded preschool programs and in federal support for state systems-building initiatives such as the Race to the Top—Early Learning Challenge program. In addition, the National Academy of Sciences produced two significant consensus reports that speak directly to issues of early childhood assessment (NRC 2008) and to the competencies needed by the early childhood workforce to support young children's learning and development (IOM & NRC 2015). Yet the early childhood field continues to struggle to reach consensus on appropriate types of assessment for young children and the optimal interpretations and uses of assessment results.

Achieving an understanding of young children's learning is deeply rooted in teachers' powers of observation. Up-close, ongoing observation and recording of what children say and do yield valuable information about their interests and emerging understandings. Teachers use this information to create rich learning environments and to implement effective instructional programs for all children (Jablon, Dombro, & Dichtelmiller 2007;

Rous & Hallam 2016). However, across the continuum of pre-K to 12, the national focus on professional accountability and quality programming has evolved into a call for more and more testing of younger and younger children.

It is reasonable to ask for evidence of how young children are developing and learning. It is also reasonable to ask if early childhood programs are providing the most appropriate and effective learning environments. However, as standardized test scores and percentile rankings compete with formative assessments and portfolios of children's work, the nature of the evidence used to answer questions about children's progress and program quality continues to be a matter of considerable debate.

As the accountability and testing debate continues, young children need advocates who are equipped with the knowledge and skills to participate in discourse that is grounded in the basic principles of sound assessment practice. Therefore, responsible early childhood educators need to reach beyond enhancing their skills in observation and documentation and move more deliberately toward developing *assessment literacy*—a deep understanding of the uses and limitations of the full range of assessment options and knowledge of the most appropriate methods to capture young children's learning and development (AERA, APA, & NCME 2014; IOM & NRC 2015; Stiggins 1991). Such methods include teachers' anecdotal notes, samples of children's drawings and constructions, and records of their conversations, as well as a variety of more formal instruments.

Assessment and Testing

Accurate assessment of young children's learning is a complicated process. The rapid, episodic learning that characterizes early childhood is a significant assessment challenge. Young children may or may not fully engage in a structured assessment task; a 4-year-old may be much more interested in telling the teacher about his family's new pet than in following a set of standardized instructions. Furthermore, young children's understandings may look different from week to week. A child's experiences outside of the classroom, such as a fishing trip with a family member, can reshape her concepts of living and nonliving things and food sources.

Although the number of screening, diagnostic, and achievement instruments has increased over the years, most norm-referenced standardized measures provide a very limited view of early learning. The full picture of learning and development often requires assessors to supplement these measures with formative assessments and observational measures of classroom quality and teacher–child interactions. (For a discussion of assessment-related terms, please see "Common Assessment Terms and How to Use Them: A Glossary for Early Childhood Educators" on pages 15–20 in this volume.)

As the tension continues between providing high-quality, developmentally appropriate instruction and using instructional time to administer and interpret standardized tests that may be disconnected from the curriculum, a fundamental distinction needs to be made between testing and the process of assessment. *Assessment* may be defined as the ongoing process of gathering evidence of learning in order to make informed judgments about instructional practice (NRC 2008). This process occurs continually in almost every early childhood classroom as teachers listen to children's conversations, ask strategic questions to probe their understanding, observe their actions, and make informed judgments about the progress of an individual child or a group of children.

In contrast, a *test* has been defined as a procedure that systematically samples behavior in a specific domain and scores it in a standardized manner (AERA, APA, & NCME 2014). Tests can provide a quick look at specific behaviors at a particular point in time. However, they produce just one type of evidence that might be gathered in the overall assessment process.

Appropriate assessment is an integral part of the teaching and learning process. Sound assessment practices can

> Highlight children's knowledge, skills, and interests

> Document children's growth over time

> Describe children's progress toward specified learning goals

> Provide constructive feedback to instructional programs and policy makers

When implemented effectively, the assessment process can be a powerful tool for teachers. By collecting a record of children's growth over time, teachers can use assessment results to advocate for what children know and are able to do when these competencies are not apparent from the results of more standardized measures. In addition, assessment results can be the centerpiece for meaningful conversations between families and educators.

Framing the Assessment Conversation

Assessment is more than a single data point. As the National Research Council's report *Early Childhood Assessment: Why, What, and How* argues,

> The selection and use of assessments, in early childhood as elsewhere, should be part of a larger system that specifies the infrastructure for distributing and delivering medical or educational services, maintaining quality, supporting professional development, distributing information, and guiding further planning and decision making. (NRC 2008, 28)

However, these complex discussions on accountability and testing can be framed around a few fundamental, critical assessment-related issues. The following questions do not represent an exhaustive set of the major issues in accountability and the testing of young children. Rather, they attempt to suggest some basic interrelated assessment concerns that teachers, administrators, and families who use assessment information should pose and be able to challenge as they participate in the accountability debate.

What Is the Purpose of Assessment?

Twenty years after the publication of *Principles and Recommendations for Early Childhood Assessments,* a report to the National Goal Panel (Shepard, Kagan, & Wurtz 1998), it remains the foundation of our understanding of the major purposes of early childhood assessment:

> Supporting learning

> Identifying special needs

> Evaluating programs and monitoring trends

> Providing high-stakes accountability

Although the primary purpose of early childhood assessment is to improve instruction and thereby support children's learning, identifying special needs and monitoring program quality are also legitimate uses. The high-stakes accountability decisions that result from some assessment data, however, must be carefully considered in the light of appropriate assessment use (AERA, APA, & NCME 2014).

A teacher who needs to gather information about particular children's progress in developing science concepts, for example, might collect the children's drawings, take photographs of their constructions, and record or document their conversations. Classroom- and curriculum-based assessments can help teachers plan more appropriate instructional practices, because these assessments are directly tied to instruction and provide a close look at individual children.

When information about individual children is not needed, evidence about the quality and effectiveness of the educational program might come from assessing a sample of children rather than an entire population. An administrator, for example, may need to collect evidence about whether an instructional program has been effective and how all children, or subgroups of children, seem to be progressing toward a set of learning goals. In this case, it may be helpful to have a sample group of children perform a comparable task that reflects the desired learning goals. The assessment data from such sampling procedures are one part of the evidence that the administrator can use to evaluate program effectiveness and monitor group progress.

Clarifying the purpose of an assessment is a preliminary step in making decisions about the

> Content and type of knowledge to be assessed

> Population to be assessed (for example, a subset of children or an entire population)

> Most appropriate assessment method and instrument

> Target audience for the assessment information—teachers, parents, policy makers, the children themselves

> Formats in which assessment results will be reported to the target audience

What Content and Type of Knowledge Is Being Assessed?

The content and type of knowledge to be assessed is critical in determining the assessment method and instrument. For example, if a teacher wants to determine how Sanjay's gross motor skills are developing, the most appropriate assessment method would be a performance assessment in which the teacher asks Sanjay to do specific gross motor tasks. Moving beyond simply identifying a curriculum domain to be assessed, such as reading or science, to aligning assessment methods with desired learning targets—what children need to know and be able to do in a particular domain—is recommended (Chappuis et al. 2012).

Understanding the type of learning target they want to assess will help educators choose the appropriate assessment method. Chappuis and colleagues (2012) identify the following types of learning targets:

> **Knowledge:** Does Madison identify a group of objects with a corresponding number?

> **Reasoning:** How does Elena go about recording her observations of the class gerbil?

> **Skills:** Can Yuan write his first name using upper- and lowercase letters?

> **Products:** Can Asia use what she knows about design to build a cardboard model of a house?

> **Dispositions:** Does Reginald often seek out books on his own and pretend to read them?

What Is the Most Appropriate Assessment Method?

Defining the assessment purpose and the content and type of knowledge to be assessed forms the groundwork for selecting the most suitable assessment method and instrument. Early childhood educators need to understand the range of appropriate assessment options, from classroom-based to norm-referenced measures, and the importance of using multiple methods of assessment.

For example, evidence of children's ability to perform a task may or may not reveal their dispositions and self-regulation skills, but having this knowledge can help teachers choose effective ways of teaching and interacting with individual children. While a student might read fluently and with comprehension, this does not, by itself, reveal the child's ability to persist when encountering an unfamiliar word or to focus attention on the text when there is a minor environmental distraction. The teacher might gather evidence of the child's reading performance by engaging her in an actual reading task and using a checklist, but gauging the child's persistence, attention, and focus may require further exploration through observation and more structured tasks.

To meet the differing assessment needs of educators, school officials, policy makers, and others, assessment must be part of a comprehensive system. The California Education Code (2014) defines a comprehensive assessment system as "a system of assessments of pupils that has the primary purposes of assisting teachers, administrators, and pupils and their parents; improving teaching and learning; and promoting high-quality teaching and learning using a variety of assessment approaches and item types" (Section 60602.5[a]). A comprehensive assessment system should include screening measures, formative assessments, and measures of the quality of both the environment and adult–child interactions (ED 2018).

How Will the Assessment Results Be Evaluated?

Samples of children's work, teachers' anecdotal notes, and performances on standardized measures are eventually evaluated against appropriate learning goals and standards, the performance of a similar group of children, or a scoring rubric. At some point an informed judgment or evaluation must be made that will modify an instructional program, generate further assessment, or provide feedback on program quality. Carefully gathered evidence is of little use unless it begins to answer questions about how young children are developing and learning and whether programs are providing the most appropriate, effective learning environments. Therefore, learning goals and standards must be appropriate, and any comparison groups must be as similar as possible to the child or group being assessed.

> Mrs. Jacobs knows that by the end of third grade, her current kindergarteners are expected to have mastered this state science standard: *Keep records that describe observations, carefully distinguish actual observations from ideas and speculation, and are understandable weeks and months later.* To support her students' development of these skills, she designs a unit on change and decay. As part of the unit, the children conduct regular, ongoing observations of two pumpkins, one of which has been split into two pieces and one of which remains intact. The children engage in group discussions about their observations of the changes occurring in the sliced pumpkin and on the outside of the intact pumpkin. They keep science journals in which they draw and write their observations and impressions. All classroom-based and formal assessment information is weighed against the children's progress toward the science standard.

Are Assessments Results Reported Clearly and Accurately?

Understanding assessment results can be daunting. The most well-constructed, appropriate assessment is useless if the intended audience—teachers, families, center directors, principals, and/or policy makers—cannot understand the results. Young children and educators are not well served when instructional and policy decisions are made on the basis of assessment results that the intended audience does not understand.

According to Standard 6.10 in *Standards for Educational and Psychological Testing,* "When test score information is released, those responsible for testing programs should provide interpretations appropriate to the audience. The interpretations should describe in simple language what the test covers, what the scores represent, and how the scores are intended to be used" (AERA, APA, & NCME 2014, 119). In addition, Standard 6.11 states, "When automatically generated interpretations of test response protocols or test performance are reported, the sources, rationale, and empirical basis for these interpretations should be available, and their limitations should be described" (119).

When Mr. Scott meets with the families of the preschoolers in his classroom to talk about the children's development, he shows them samples of their children's drawings, their constructions, and transcripts of conversations he has collected over time. He discusses the children's work in the context of trajectories for typical development while acknowledging each child's specific patterns of learning. The children's work samples frame the conversations with families about how their children's learning is progressing and what the next stages of development might look like.

How Are the Assessment Results to Be Used?

Perhaps the most important element of any assessment is the ultimate use of the assessment information. Use of the data to make decisions—such as extending a lesson for a few additional days, identifying a child as needing special services, or providing additional resources to a program—should be linked to the stated purpose of the assessment process, aligned to intended use of the assessment method or instrument, and based on a thorough understanding of the assessment results. Applying assessment results should cause no harm.

Conclusion

No assessment, by itself, can improve the quality of instruction or enhance children's outcomes. Rather, assessment data can and should serve as a catalyst for continuous quality improvement. The assessment issues described in this article are basic to a reasoned discourse on accountability and testing of young children. If the conversation is based on principles of sound measurement practice, the fields of early childhood education and educational measurement will be challenged in new ways to act as responsible advocates for children.

The Institute of Medicine and National Research Council report (IOM & NRC 2015) outlines a set of competencies that are important for all early childhood educators who work with children from birth through age 8. These include the following understandings related to assessment:

> **Core knowledge base:** Knowledge of principles for assessing children that are developmentally appropriate; culturally sensitive; and relevant, reliable, and valid across a variety of populations, domains, and assessment purposes

> **Practices to help children learn:** Ability to select, employ, and interpret a portfolio of both informal and formal assessment tools and strategies; to use the results to understand individual children's developmental progression and determine whether needs are being met; and to use this information to individualize, adapt, and improve instructional practices (328–29)

Those in leadership and administrative roles also need the following competencies related to assessing children (IOM & NRC 2015):

> Knowledge of assessment principles and methods to monitor children's progress and ability to adjust practice accordingly

> Ability to select assessment tools for use by the professionals in their setting (344)

Culturally and Linguistically Appropriate Assessment

The assessment of young children is, by its very nature, a culturally and linguistically loaded interaction. This must be acknowledged and understood at a deep level. Consider, for example, the following factors surrounding any situation in which a child's learning is being assessed.

Teacher characteristics. Teachers observe and document young children's learning through the lens of their own personal and professional experiences. Because no one is naturally blind to differences in color, race, gender, socioeconomic status, and other personal characteristics, educators must combine a deep understanding of child development with personal introspection to mitigate the implicit biases that can skew their interpretation of children's behavior.

Child characteristics. Children grow and develop in the context of their families and communities, and they, like teachers, bring their own unique set of experiences to any assessment setting. For example, the language used to communicate with a child as well as that used by the child to demonstrate his knowledge and skills are critical variables in accurately discerning the child's abilities. When a child does not fully understand the language used by an adult in an assessment situation, it should not be surprising that the child's performance appears to be poor. Further, when the adult does not fully understand the language of a child she is assessing, accurately documenting and evaluating the child's conversation and writing may not be possible.

Test characteristics. Standardized, norm-referenced measures are often viewed as benefiting some groups while disadvantaging others because of the focus of test items or the language of the assessment. Nuanced distinctions that can favor one subgroup over another must be explored and addressed. The purpose of assessment instruments is to differentiate among those with varying degrees of knowledge, skills, and dispositions around a specific topic. However, achieving fairness in any assessment context requires an assurance that the results differentiate by competence in the domain that is assessed rather than by racial or ethnic subgroup, gender, or socioeconomic status. Without such assurance, the fairness of the assessment is in doubt, and there can be little confidence in the interpretation of the results. Achieving fairness is not easy. The individual test items presented on a standardized assessment cannot have precisely the same familiarity to all students. This is why it is so important that an assessment be used with children who are similar to the population on whom the test was normed.

A completely culture-free test would be very difficult to construct; even a nonverbal test would have some cultural components. However, it is critical for educators and officials working in districts and state educational offices to understand how factors unrelated to the purpose of a test may affect the way it is administered, how children perform, and how the results are interpreted and used.

And early childhood teacher preparation programs have the opportunity and the challenge to enhance their assessment-related content so that candidates have a repertoire of assessment strategies and the knowledge and skills needed for accurate use and interpretation of assessment data.

All educators can become better advocates for young children when they are able to demystify assessment and testing and understand the strengths and limitations of the range of assessment options. As educators build their assessment literacy, they can inform families and hold policy makers responsible for supporting sound assessment practices for young children and the programs that serve them.

Reflection Questions

1. Why does assessment matter?

2. How might you explain the difference between assessment and tests to a colleague or child's family?

3. This article mentions a number of benefits of assessment. What other benefits can you identify or have you seen for children in your own program?

4. Consider the ways you currently assess the different types of knowledge and skills children are expected to have and do. What barriers have you encountered? What solutions could you implement to overcome these barriers?

5. How do you use the information you gather about children's learning and development to inform your practice? In what ways might you make even more meaningful connections between assessment and instruction?

References

AERA (American Educational Research Association), APA (American Psychological Association), & NCME (National Council on Measurement in Education). 2014. *Standards for Educational and Psychological Testing.* Washington, DC: AERA.

Chappuis, J., R.J. Stiggins, S. Chappuis, & J.A. Arter. 2012. *Classroom Assessment for Student Learning: Doing It Right—Using It Well.* 2nd ed. Upper Saddle River, NJ: Pearson.

ED (US Department of Education). 2018. "Definitions." Accessed January 14. www.ed.gov/early-learning/elc-draft-summary/definitions.

IOM (Institute of Medicine) & (NRC) National Research Council. 2015. *Transforming the Workforce for Children Birth Through 8: A Unifying Foundation.* Washington, DC: National Academies Press.

Jablon, J.R., A.L. Dombro, & M.L. Dichtelmiller. 2007. *The Power of Observation: Birth to Age Eight.* 2nd ed. Washington, DC: Teaching Strategies.

Jones, J. 2004. "Framing the Assessment Discussion." *Young Children* 59 (1): 14–18.

NRC (National Research Council). 2008. *Early Childhood Assessment: Why, What, and How.* Washington, DC: National Academies Press. doi:10.17226/12446.

Rous, B., & R. Hallam. 2016. "Screening and Supporting Children at Risk for Developmental Delay or Disability." In *The Leading Edge of Early Childhood Education: Linking Science to Policy for a New Generation,* eds. N.K. Lesaux & S.M. Jones, 117–34. Cambridge, MA: Harvard Education Press.

Shepard, L., S.L. Kagan, & E. Wurtz, eds. 1998. *Principles and Recommendations for Early Childhood Assessments.* Washington, DC: National Education Goals Panel.

Stiggins, R.J. 1991. "Assessment Literacy." *Phi Delta Kappan* 72 (7): 534–39.

About the Author

Jacqueline Jones, PhD, is president and CEO of the Foundation for Child Development. She served as the country's first deputy assistant secretary for Policy and Early Learning in the US Department of Education and was the assistant commissioner for the Division of Early Childhood Education in the New Jersey State Department of Education.

Common Assessment Terms and How to Use Them

A Glossary for Early Childhood Educators

Elena Bodrova and Deborah J. Leong

Although *assessment* has become a loaded word in the field of early childhood education—often associated with bias, push-down expectations that are not developmentally appropriate, and pressure on children and teachers to perform—appropriate, authentic assessment lies at the heart of learning and teaching. It enables educators to better understand an individual child, build on her strengths, and respond to her needs in the classroom. It is only when teachers have an accurate picture of what each child knows and is able to do that they can build joyful, responsive, caring classrooms.

Early childhood teachers use assessment for a variety of reasons, including

› Determining a child's progress, both individually and as part of a group

› Making adjustments to instruction to support children's learning

› Communicating information about children's learning and development to others, such as families, administrators, and specialists

› Contributing to schools' and programs' accountability reports required by federal, state, and local laws and regulations (McAfee, Leong, & Bodrova 2016)

Collecting objective, detailed information in respectful, nonbiased, and accurate ways is critical to assessment being fair and useful for classroom decision making (Jiban 2013). Much of the observation and assessment in early childhood classrooms is informal and happens daily. This frequent information gathering, carried out during routines the children are familiar with, builds a picture of each child's learning and leads to changes in the way teachers support and interact with children. For example, after several observations of the children in your classroom during center time, you notice that Seamus chooses to play only in the block center. Wanting to use this interest to encourage Seamus to explore new learning opportunities, you decide to add building materials to other learning centers.

New education initiatives, evolving terminology, and the needs of all the diverse learners in your classroom will introduce you to new or updated terms related to standards and assessment. Keeping up with these changes in language is an essential component of being an effective educator. This glossary will help teachers navigate key words used in the world of early childhood assessment and better understand the uses of various types of assessments.

Glossary of Terms

accommodation: An approved change or adjustment in an assessment procedure to yield more accurate information for some children, such as administering an assessment in a dual language learner's home language or providing more time for a child with a disability to complete the assessment. When accommodations are made, the assessment measure itself remains unchanged, meaning that a child's performance will be judged against the same standards as the child's peers.

accountability: The responsibility of an educator or an educational institution (a school or a center) for students' learning outcomes.

achievement test: A test, typically standardized and norm referenced, designed to measure how much a child has learned in school; this may be specific to a content area (e.g., reading or math) or more general.

alignment: *Horizontal alignment* is the agreement between student outcomes (such as those stated in early learning standards and guidelines), curricula, and assessment. *Vertical alignment* refers to the continuity of expectations for student learning from one educational level (e.g., grade) to another.

alternative assessment: An assessment given to a child with a disability that uses different standards for mastery than assessments given to the child's peers; previously referred to as *modifications*.

aptitude test: A test, typically standardized, intended to predict a child's future performance based on his current learning and ability. For example, aptitude tests may be used as a measure of a child's kindergarten readiness (readiness tests) or to determine a child's eligibility for a gifted program.

artifact: A tangible item from children's work and play that gives evidence of learning, such as a drawing, painting, writing sample, block building, or graph.

assessment: The process of gathering information from several forms of evidence (e.g., observations, tests, work samples), which is then compiled, analyzed, and interpreted to evaluate a child's learning and development.

authentic assessment: Conducted as part of a child's ongoing participation in an educational setting with tasks as close as possible to the child's real-life experiences.

benchmark: A clearly defined expectation of what children should know and be able to do by a specific point in their learning and development, typically tied to age or grade level. For example, by the end of preschool, children may be expected to understand the differences between letters, numbers, and words. A benchmark can be divided into more specific expectations, called *indicators*.

bias: Any characteristic of an assessment that unfairly discriminates against or favors a child or group of children on the basis of factors such as gender, urban or rural residence, socioeconomic class, race, ethnicity, culture, or language.

classroom assessment: An ongoing process developed and used by teachers to identify the strengths, needs, and progress of the children in their classrooms and to inform their teaching.

Common Core State Standards (CCSS): A set of K–12 mathematics and English language arts/literacy standards that specify what children should know and be able to do by the end of each grade; these standards were developed by the Common Core State Standards Initiative and are consistent across all states that adopt them (CCSS Initiative 2018).

criterion-referenced test: A standardized instrument in which a child's performance is compared to a pre-specified standard, such as a cutoff score or a level of skill or content mastery. For example, in a kindergarten reading assessment, by the end of the school year children may be expected to be able to read a book of a certain level of difficulty and answer comprehension questions about it.

curriculum-based assessment: A process in which children's performance is evaluated against objectives contained in a specific curriculum.

diagnostic assessment: An in-depth evaluation of an individual child by a specialist to determine whether the child has a particular cognitive or language delay or deficit or a behavior disorder; usually performed after a child has been referred by a teacher, physician, or family member or if a concern is identified in the course of screening.

documentation: The process of gathering evidence and artifacts of children's learning, which may include work samples, observations, anecdotal records, and transcripts of children's conversations.

early learning standards and guidelines: A set of expectations for the learning and development of young children across the domains of physical health and motor development, social and emotional development, language and literacy development, cognitive development, and approaches to learning.

formal assessment: A process for obtaining information about children's learning and development, typically for the purpose of reporting to others. Often involves specific requirements, such as uniform criteria for administration, scoring, and interpretation for all children; administration may be required on a specific schedule determined by the school, district, or state. Examples vary from classroom assessments that use a specific set of scoring rubrics to standardized tests.

formative assessment: A process teachers use to monitor and provide feedback on children's learning and to adjust their own instruction to better meet children's needs.

high-stakes assessment: A process used to inform important educational decisions made about programs, teachers, or children. It might, for example, influence specific learning decisions for a child, such as retention in a grade or placement in a specific program.

indicator: The most specific description of an expected outcome for a child (e.g., "identifies uppercase and lowercase letters in a grouping of letters and numerals"); also evidence that documents children's attainment of a specific level of a benchmark or standard.

informal assessment: A process for obtaining information about children's learning and development using nonstandardized procedures (e.g., observation, portfolio assessment) and flexible schedules; typically used for formative purposes, such as making classroom decisions about how to individualize an activity, rather than for decisions such as determining an individual child's kindergarten readiness.

Next Generation Science Standards (NGSS): A set of K–12 science standards that specify what children should know and be able to do by the end of each grade across the domains of physical sciences, life science, earth and space science, and engineering design; these standards are consistent across all states that adopt them (NGSS 2018).

norm-referenced test: A standardized process in which a child's performance is interpreted by comparing it to the performance of a group of peers, or *norming group,* who have previously taken the same test. It is important that a test was normed on children who are similar to those taking the test, and assessors must be aware of potential bias and limitations of tests and their results.

observational assessment: A process based on teachers' observation of children's behavior. It can be open ended, such as when a teacher watches a child explore and interact in the classroom to learn about her interests, choice of friends, and likes and dislikes, among other things. Or the process may be more structured, such as through the use of a preset scale or rubric for a teacher to specifically record what he observes (e.g., "Paolo volunteers comments and information during group time," "Thea follows three-step directions").

outcome: A description of knowledge or skills a child is expected to demonstrate in a certain area of development; also called *learning outcome.* In early childhood education, *outcome* is used similarly to how the term *standard* is used in K–12 education.

performance-based assessment: A strategy designed to include tasks that directly reveal children's knowledge, understanding, and skills in a targeted area; typically includes journals, portfolios, investigations, demonstrations, written or oral responses, and exhibitions. For example, a series of drawings a child made while listening to a story may be used as an assessment of this child's understanding of important events in the story.

portfolio: A collection of children's work samples and other indicators of learning collected over time; a valuable source for authentic assessment when the teacher follows a system for selecting and evaluating its contents.

program standards: A set of expectations, set by a local, state, or national agency, for the characteristics of early childhood programs necessary to ensure children's positive experiences and learning; can include structural parameters (e.g., adult–child ratio, teacher education), quality of learning environment, and/or the quality of adult–child interactions, as well as other characteristics.

referral: The recommendation that a child receive further diagnostic evaluation or special services.

reliability: The extent to which any assessment technique yields results that are accurate and consistent over time.

rubric: A guide that describes specific criteria for determining different levels of children's learning and development; particularly useful for maintaining consistency when assessing multiple work samples across different children.

sampling: Assessing a part of the population instead of the entire population, or a part of a domain of learning instead of the entire domain.

screening: A brief, standardized procedure used to determine children's health and/or developmental concerns that may impact their learning. When such concerns are detected, children are referred for further assessment.

standardized test: An assessment instrument that is administered, scored, and interpreted in a regulated manner and is developed and used according to APA/AERA/NCME guidelines (AERA, APA, & NCME 2014). It may be norm referenced or criterion referenced. It's important to remember that standardized tests are normed on specific populations and should be used only with similar populations.

standards: Expectations for children's learning (typically described as *early learning standards and guidelines*) or for the quality of a program (known as *program standards*).

summative assessment: An evaluation that takes place at the end of a specific time period or a unit of study to determine the degree of children's achievement of learning objectives; results are often used to report on children's progress to others (e.g., families, administrators).

test: A systematic procedure used to evaluate the abilities, aptitudes, skills, or performance of an individual child or a group of children; typically used as a means of formal assessment.

validity: The extent to which an assessment measures what we want to measure and not something else. An assessment is considered "valid" if the results agree with other information gathered in other ways about the same behavior.

References

AERA (American Educational Research Association), APA (American Psychological Association), & NCME (National Council on Measurement in Education). 2014. *Standards for Educational and Psychological Testing*. Washington, DC: AERA.

CCSS Initiative (Common Core State Standards Initiative). 2018. "About the Standards." Accessed March 2. www.corestandards.org/about-the-standards.

Jiban, C. 2013. *Early Childhood Assessment: Implementing Effective Practice*. A Research-Based Guide to Inform Assessment Planning in the Early Grades. http://info.nwea.org/rs/nwea/images /EarlyChildhoodAssessment-ImplementingEffectivePractice.pdf. Portland, OR: NWEA.

McAfee, O., D.J. Leong, & E. Bodrova. 2016. *Assessing and Guiding Young Children's Development and Learning*. 6th ed. Upper Saddle River, NJ: Pearson.

NGSS (Next Generation Science Standards). 2018. "Get to Know." Accessed March 2. www.nextgenscience.org.

About the Authors

Elena Bodrova, PhD, is cofounder and director of research at Tools of the Mind. Previously, she was a principal researcher at McREL International for 14 years. She is coauthor of *Assessing and Guiding Young Children's Development and Learning*, in its 6th edition, and of *Basics of Assessment: A Primer for Early Childhood Educators*.

Deborah J. Leong, PhD, is cofounder and executive director of Tools of the Mind and professor emerita of psychology at Metropolitan State University of Denver, where she taught for 36 years. She is coauthor of *Assessing and Guiding Young Children's Development and Learning* and of *Basics of Assessment: A Primer for Early Childhood Educators*.

Appropriate and Meaningful Assessment in Family-Centered Programs

James Elicker and Mary Benson McMullen

Developmentally appropriate assessment with infants and toddlers is an ongoing process teachers engage in daily, throughout the relationship with an infant or toddler, as they observe, document, reflect on, and then discuss with the family how to best support their child's development (NAEYC 2003; Zero to Three 2010). Appropriate assessment often includes conversations with families, anecdotal observations, portfolios, and more structured assessment tools.

Appropriate assessment of infants and toddlers is strengths based, identifying and building on children's capabilities, not what they cannot do, and is not used to "label" them (Moreno & Klute 2011). Meaningful assessment helps teachers and families focus on children's individual rates of development, temperaments, interests, and preferences, while also taking into account families' goals and expectations and the broader norms and values of communities and cultures (Gonzalez-Mena & Stonehouse 2008).

Continuous assessment of infants and toddlers makes use of multiple and varied types of information. It is based on deep knowledge gained about the whole child in the contexts of early care and education settings and the child's family (Moreno & Klute 2011). Teachers are creating something like a biographical documentary, addressing the questions, "Who is this child, and who has she become over time?"

Regular, ongoing assessment occurs as a natural part of day-to-day life in the caregiving environment, as teachers interact with, observe, and celebrate the accomplishments of the infants and toddlers in their care (HighScope 2018; Moreno & Klute 2011). This article discusses elements that make up continuous assessment, including ways teachers can collect, document, organize, and maintain information; the importance of reflecting on this information in collaboration with colleagues and families; and how to use this information for setting goals and planning for individual children and groups.

Collecting and Documenting Information

It takes time and effort to record observations of infants' and toddlers' experiences and the interactions with the teacher and others in early care and education environments. With careful advance planning, however, it can be something that fits easily into the daily routine. The following are some general ways teachers can collect and record information.

Anecdotal Observations

Teachers have many ways to record details of caregiving—small anecdotes and significant milestones in children's development that they see in the classroom and that families share with them. Some carry notepads or sticky notes to jot down and date brief comments to expand on later, when they have time; others record information on dry erase boards or chalkboards strategically hung around the room. Some teachers find it disruptive to take notes when they are with the children and prefer to record observations about key events when children are napping or during their break.

In addition to recording caregiving routines such as when the child was fed, how much she ate, when her diaper was changed, and when and how long she slept, teachers typically record highlights and key events of each child's day. For instance, a teacher may note that a toddler particularly enjoyed painting at the easel side by side with her friend, looking from her own paper to her friend's several times and vocalizing excitedly.

Journals and Blogs

Many teachers keep a daily or weekly journal to record their thoughts, consider discussions held with families and colleagues, reflect on their teaching, and sketch out plans for individual children and the group, the environment, and the curriculum. Family journals can be highly effective as well. Teachers can send home inexpensive spiral notebooks about once a week with photos, stories, samples of a child's work, or other important information. In turn, families return these journals with questions or short descriptions of experiences from home. For example, families may send photos of their child's first trip to the zoo, or perhaps provide comments or questions related to the work sample the teacher included in the journal that week.

If families have access to the internet, teachers can use blogs and other interactive media such as apps for sharing information about individual infants and toddlers. Teachers can upload their reflections, as well as pictures and videos, connect families directly to important resources, and have online conversations with families. Teachers can set up blogs that are private between users—family members and teachers—and deny general public access, but they must do all they can to ensure confidentiality by using secure settings and privacy features on blog sites.

Photo Documentation

Digital cameras, including pocket cameras and cell phones, have become a popular tool for documentation in infant and toddler rooms. Some teachers for example, use photos they've taken throughout the week to create a poster that highlights an important experience for each child in the class. Photos convey a lot of information, and the images delight children and family members. However, teachers should ensure that the technology used in documentation enhances the ability to communicate the accomplishments of children, and does not substitute for personal interaction between teachers and families or teachers and children. Photos and videos are also effective tools for reflective practice, as Julia Luckenbill (2012) discusses in an issue of *Young Children* (see "Taking Photos and Videos to Support Reflective Practice" on page 24).

Developmental Screening

This type of screening uses standardized instruments. These tests are normalized—that is, they have reported averages based on large and diverse groups of children (Meisels, Wen, & Beachy-Quick 2010). Screenings are designed to identify children who may have significant developmental delays or disabilities. For instance, medical practitioners screen length, weight, and head circumference to make sure an infant is growing. Hearing and vision tests or verbal and receptive language screenings are commonly used as well (OHS 2011). Screening checklists can include items like "The child points to and names familiar objects—(Always/Sometimes/Never)." Screenings may be completed by parents or teachers, medical or social

Examples of Screening and Assessment Tools

Developmental Screening Instruments

› **Ages & Stages Questionnaires (ASQ):** Family-completed developmental and social and emotional screening checklists with items for children 1 month to 5½ years. www.brookespublishing.com/resource-center/screening-and-assessment/asq

› **BRIGANCE Early Childhood Screens III:** Teacher-administered screen for children birth to 6 years that covers language, motor, self-help, social and emotional, and cognitive skills. www.curriculumassociates.com/products/detail.aspx?Title=BrigEC-Screens3

› **Parents' Evaluation of Developmental Status (PEDS):** Evidence-based screening tool for children birth to 8 years that addresses parents' concerns about development, behavior, and mental health. www.pedstest.com

Structured Assessment Tools

› **Assessment, Evaluation, and Programming System for Infants and Young Children (AEPS):** A linked system that provides teachers with skills to observe children birth to 6 years (gross motor, fine motor, adaptive, cognitive, communication, and social) and curriculum ideas to meet identified needs. http://aepslinkedsystem.com

› **BRIGANCE Inventory of Early Development III, Early Childhood Edition (IED III):** Teacher-administered assessment tool for children birth to 7 years that covers physical development, language, literacy, mathematics and science, social and emotional development, and daily living. www.curriculumassociates.com/products/detail.aspx?Title=BrigEC-IED3

› **The Ounce Scale:** Observational scale for children birth to 3½ years, for use by professionals to inform parents and monitor development, including personal connections, feelings about self, relationships with other children, understanding and communicating, exploration and problem solving, and movement and coordination. www.pearsonclinical.com/childhood/products/100000403/ounce-scale-the.html?pid=PAaOunce&Community=CA_Ed_AI_Early

› **Teaching Strategies GOLD:** Ongoing observational system for children birth through 6 years with research-based objectives in 10 areas of learning and development, including English language acquisition. https://teachingstrategies.com/solutions/assess/gold

Taking Photos and Videos to Support Reflective Practice

> Before photographing or recording children or staff, obtain written permission from families and staff. Be sensitive to their cultural views. Remember, there are many ways to observe, document, and reflect without photography.

> Let adults and children know why you take photos or record videos. You might explain to curious children that you're taking pictures of how they play and learn to show their families. Some teachers may feel a bit self-consciousness when the camera is on them. Assure them that you're trying to find moments when they are engaged with the children and when children demonstrate milestones. Explain that photos often create opportunities for discussion and reflection.

> Carefully and thoughtfully observe interactions between children and teachers before you attempt to take any photographs. Being intentional will help you develop an eye for teachable moments and help you capture them successfully.

> Make sure you have quick access to your camera. When teachable moments happen, leaving to retrieve your camera might mean missing key interactions that make for the ideal photograph.

> Seek images where the child and teacher are sharing a special moment. Zoom in on their faces and look for reciprocal exchanges. Well-photographed moments can lead to conversations with the teacher about the interaction.

> Begin by capturing positive interactions between children and teachers. Once you have built a trusting relationship with a new teacher, you can explore with her the possibility of photographing more challenging situations.

(From Luckenbill 2012)

service providers, or early intervention professionals. (See "Examples of Screening and Assessment Tools" on page 23.) Whether or not screening identifies a possible delay or disability, it can provide a starting point for discussions with the family about the child's strengths, interests, and needs. If caregivers suspect a child has a particular challenge, they should discuss it with the family and consider together whether to refer the child to the appropriate professional for formal evaluation (OHS 2011).

Structured Assessment

Another assessment method is the use of a criterion-referenced developmental scale to monitor children's progress. The most effective structured assessments are not "tests" teachers administer to all children the same way but are instead authentic assessments that rely on daily observations of children's typical activities at home and in care. (See "Examples of Screening and Assessment Tools" on page 23.) The teacher uses anecdotal observations as reported by families to note the emergence of children's behaviors and skills included in the scale. Tracking each child's social and emotional, self-help, language, cognitive, and physical development through these types of assessments helps teachers collaborate with families, celebrate new milestones, and plan appropriate and challenging learning experiences for individual children. For example, a mother reports her 10-month-old son really seems to "follow her gaze" and pay attention when she points to the bird feeder outside the kitchen window, signaling to the teachers that the baby is ready to attend more closely to objects teachers point out and label in board books and on daily buggy rides.

Before using a structured assessment tool, program directors and teachers should examine it carefully together, ensuring and better understanding how the skills measured are a good match with the program's philosophy for children and families. For example, teachers can make sure the skills listed in the assessment are ones considered important by the program and its families. They can also ensure the skills are observable in the child's everyday activities at home and in the program.

Organizing and Maintaining Records

For daily record keeping, simple systems such as individual expandable file folders, bins, boxes, or baskets labeled for each child are handy for depositing anecdotal records, notes, photos, and structured screening or assessment forms. Some teachers prefer large binders with pockets and plastic sleeves for collecting and maintaining daily reports and information. Increasingly, teachers are combining physical paper records with electronic systems.

Periodically, caregivers need to take what they've learned and all of the loose bits of information they have collected and put it all together in a meaningful way to share with others. Sometimes this is in preparation for conferences with families or perhaps to prepare documentation for accreditation or another required report. Portfolios and developmental profiles are the most common forms for pulling all of the information together for individual infants and toddlers (Jarrett, Browne, & Wallin 2006). Teachers can use online resources as well as books to help guide them in portfolio construction.

Portfolios

Portfolios support a strengths-based approach to assessment by serving as a means to collect and showcase children's abilities. "Portfolios may contain collections of representative work of children that illustrate their progress and achievements" (Gestwicki 2010, 304). Teachers can use a variety of formats to create portfolios—boxes, binders, or electronic files—but the important thing is that each portfolio is unique in telling the story of an individual child. Items teachers typically put in portfolios include the following:

> Carefully selected photographs

> Audio and video recordings of children playing and experiencing life indoors and outdoors

> Samples of children's language and work, such as paintings, scribbles, and collages of leaves, pebbles, and twigs

> Teacher reflections

> Screening and assessment reports

Developmental Profiles

Developmentally appropriate practice reminds us to look at the whole child, not just isolated abilities or areas of development (Copple & Bredekamp 2009). It is useful, however, to organize observations and records around commonly recognized areas of development and learning for this age period. Observations, anecdotal records, and communications are often broken down into manageable parts or categories, such as social and emotional development; physical development; development of communication, language, and literacy; cognitive development and the development of critical thinking skills; and the development of self-help and personal care skills.

Developmental profiles provide a framework for organizing the various pieces of evidence (e.g., anecdotal notes, reflections, assessment results) collected by teachers to help them describe a child's progress across several developmental categories over a period of time (CDE 2015). Teachers in high-quality infant and toddler programs typically compile developmental profiles for each child two or three times each year to share in conferences with families. Teachers and families discuss this document and use it to collaborate on goal setting. (See page 27 for an example of a developmental profile.)

Collaboration and Reflection

Family-centered infant and toddler teachers form partnerships with families in supporting healthy and positive outcomes for their children (Dunst, Bruder, & Espe-Sherwindt 2014). Partnership is the key—it is a true working collaboration in which the expertise of families is respected. Making time for reflection, as well as communicating, is central to this collaborative relationship.

Teachers can support this collaboration by taking time to reflect on information gathered about the infants and toddlers in their care. Processing thoughts about observations, interactions, and experiences over time allows various pieces of the puzzle to fall into place. Initial conclusions and beliefs formed when observing children—ideas about what a teacher sees and understands—need to be discussed openly with colleagues and, even more important, with families (Gonzalez-Mena & Stonehouse 2008; Zero to Three 2010).

For example, it is important for teachers to hold formal conferences a minimum of two or three times each year for teachers and families to share information. Teachers also can make the most of daily drop-off and pickup times by asking questions and sharing information with families and inviting feedback, especially as such an exchange impacts immediate goal setting and plans for individualized care.

All who engage in collaborative reflection benefit from sharing information about an individual infant or toddler—or the group as a whole. Missing pieces of knowledge are filled in, incorrect assumptions corrected, and alternative conclusions generated—and everyone comes away feeling part of the decision making. This critical part of the assessment process respects the multiple concerns and perspectives of all of those who are part of the infant and toddler caregiving team.

For example, a family might ask teachers to support their efforts to potty train their 1-year-old. Instead of rejecting the request or making a culturally based assumption that "no 1-year-olds can do this," the teachers can engage in a discussion with the family to find out why it is so important to them. Teachers might discover that the family is returning soon to their home country, where the baby will be expected to have this skill, and they fear embarrassment. After a discussion with the family about their method of supporting early toilet learning, the family and teachers can consider how to adapt and incorporate toilet learning into group care for their child.

Selected Excerpts from a Developmental Profile Assessment for a Family Conference for Bailey, Age 2½ Years

This developmental profile is based on information gained from screenings and shared by the family, anecdotal records and journal entries (from teachers and family), captioned photos, and daily reports about activities such as eating and toileting.

Social and Emotional Development: Understanding of self and others; the development of responsibility, interpersonal skills, and the management of emotions.

Bailey is very social and displays many prosocial skills. We've seen empathy in the way he reacts when children are crying; he often asks, "They OK?" Although he still prefers to play with materials (particularly trains) undisturbed, he'll seek out interactions with peers, as when he engaged in playing dress-up with two friends. He's often heard explaining that "my mommy come back, my daddy come back," a phrase that other children repeat using Bailey's speech patterns. Bailey follows along very comfortably with familiar routines and rules, and is not thrown off by the unexpected, as demonstrated during a recent tornado drill.

Development of Critical Thinking Skills: Ability/persistence in problem solving, desire to learn, creative expression (art, movement), mathematic skills, scientific inquiry; enjoyment in learning.

Bailey has shown much development in his critical thinking skills since beginning in our program. He loves to explore, such as using the magnifying glass to look at "big bugs." His emerging mathematical skills are a clear example of this—he loves to line up cars and point to each one, counting quietly to himself. He groups objects by concrete similarities, and the attributes he uses for grouping are becoming more complex (first similar objects, then similar function). For example, he recently lined up the wooden people and matched different sets of people. Also, he works with puzzles, using trial and error to problem solve. Often Bailey's first instinct is to cry out to get an adult to fix a problem for him. Teachers and parents can encourage Bailey's problem solving by encouraging him to work through problems, providing suggestions and emotional support.

Physical Skills Development: Use and storage of sensory information; physical stability and control of large and small muscles.

Bailey shows above average physical development for his age. When Bailey is familiar with materials and surroundings, he freely explores sensory materials and is comfortable working with messy materials such as paint and shaving cream. In new situations he uses familiar caregivers to assist him in regulating sensory input, like when the class watched the construction site outside of the playground fence and the teachers needed to help Bailey manage his fear of the large equipment and loud noise. He is at ease using his hands and fingers to do messy, fine motor activities such as using squirt bottles, pinching the bulb of the eyedropper, squeezing and shaping modeling clay, and hammering pegs. He demonstrates physical stability, jumping off the small loft and landing on his feet and walking around the bike track pushing a stroller.

Development of Self-Help and Personal Care Skills: Capacity to take care of personal needs; acquiring age-appropriate independence when eating, toileting, dressing, and completing hygiene tasks.

Bailey demonstrates competence in several key personal care skills. First, he has completed all major self-feeding tasks for a child his age. He takes bites and chews food with his mouth closed, drinks from an open cup without spilling, and successfully uses utensils without spilling food. He assists in dressing himself and there are pieces of clothing like hats that he is capable of putting on and taking off without help. Bailey also shows competence in the care of his hands, face, and nose, and he participates in frequent hand washing and the use of tissues when necessary. Last, while Bailey does not show the interest in toilet use at school that he does at home, he willingly participates in diaper changes.

Development of Communication, Language, and Literacy: Ability to communicate effectively with words, signs, and symbols; enjoyment/use of printed materials.

Bailey has shown considerable growth in his vocabulary and use of language over this past year. Nine months ago, he was speaking in one- and two-word sentences. For instance, he would stand at the sink in the bathroom and ask for "more" and point at the paper towel dispenser. Now Bailey tells complete stories and will readily talk to the teachers about what he needs.

Activities that he has participated in, like blowing bubbles and singing, have helped support his fluency and build his vocabulary and expressive language skills. He can also do these activities at home. Bailey also shows an interest in printed material. He frequently requests to be read to and participates in group story times (he loves it when we listen to the audiobook, *The Ants Go Marching!*). He looks at books independently, and he knows the purpose and proper use of writing materials.

Conclusion

Overall, Bailey shows many skills expected of a 2½-year-old. He is interested in peers and seeks out interactions with them. He shows a desire to learn, pursuing his own interests as well as participating in planned activities. He engages in many literacy activities, such as reading independently and with teachers, and uses writing tools like markers and crayons. He often practices the use of self-care skills like attempts at toileting or hand washing. Bailey displays creativity in terms of his art, body movements, and imaginative play as well as engaging in many math skills, like sorting and matching. Based on teacher observations and the reporting tool developed by the state Department of Education to help guide understanding of development, Bailey displays average and above average skills for a child his age in all skill areas.

Culturally and Linguistically Appropriate Assessment

As infant–toddler programs serve families that are increasingly diverse, how do early childhood professionals develop ways of assessing children that are individually, developmentally, and culturally appropriate? Effectively communicating and engaging with families are critical components of assessment, but these can be challenging tasks when serving families from multiple cultural and linguistic backgrounds. Here are a few ideas for building positive, effective relationships with the families in your program:

Make all families feel welcome. How does your program make efforts to welcome all families and help them feel comfortable? Are there welcoming spaces and messages in families' home languages, with comfortable places to have conversations? Finding ways for families to feel at home with the program will pay off as teachers begin to gather and share assessment information about infants and toddlers and as they work with families to set goals for the future.

Involve a staff member or volunteer who speaks the family's home language. Whether you are sharing your observations of a child with her family or asking the family to complete a screening form at home, it is essential that the language used is mutually understood. Conversing in the language most comfortable for families can help to avoid misunderstandings and confusion as information about the child is gathered and exchanged.

Offer to conduct home visits. Home visits can be a useful way to open lines of communication and make families feel more at ease. While some families might be reluctant or apprehensive about the idea of a home visit, others feel more secure and confident talking with educators about their children in a familiar environment. Visiting a family's home also provides educators with a valuable opportunity to learn more about their routines, communication styles, and childrearing practices, information that can be used to inform assessment and teaching decisions.

Collaborate. An important part of the assessment process is working together with a family to develop goals for their child. Collaborative goal setting should be seen as a process that occurs regularly rather than as a one-time event. Teachers and families may not always agree on the importance of goals for the child, and these differences in values and perspectives are even more common when educators and families have different cultural backgrounds. The keys to finding common ground are to respectfully listen, keep the two-way conversation going, and make every attempt to both understand and make understood the reasons for each opinion (Gonzalez-Mena & Stonehouse 2008). Sometimes a reasonable compromise is possible; other times, the teacher will come to understand and agree with the family's goal or vice versa. Ultimately, collaboration between teachers and families is all about working together to do what is best for the child.

Supporting Children with Delays or Disabilities

Developmentally appropriate assessment is vital to meeting the unique needs of infants and toddlers who have a delay or disability. Here are a few things to keep in mind as you observe and assess children with identified or potential delays or disabilities.

› Use a strengths-based approach. This is critical when observing and assessing infants and toddlers with delays or disabilities. It is often easier to focus on what a child *isn't* doing compared to her peers or to developmental milestone charts than it is to see what that child *can* do in a given context.

› You may need to observe a child with a disability more often, or in a greater variety of situations, than you typically might to get a full picture of the skills she's developed.

› When you share your observations with a child's family, think about what the family has identified as important to their child's development. Are they most eager to hear about their toddler's language development? Then focus your anecdotal notes or video documentation on times when she's making sounds or gesturing to communicate her needs.

› Look for guidance from the publisher when using structured assessments and screening tools to assess children who have already been identified as having a delay or disability. In some cases, the tool itself is used to identify potential delays. If your assessment reveals a potential concern with a child's development, be prepared to share that information with his family in a dignified and supportive way.

Planning and Goal Setting

Planning and preparing new experiences, both for individual infants and toddlers and for the group, are the final key elements of ongoing assessment. The shared conclusions that teachers and families reach through ongoing assessment and collaborative relationships help them define goals. Using a thorough assessment process with multiple inputs and perspectives ensures that new experiences are based on reasonable expectations and will be at a pace appropriate for each child (Gonzalez-Mena & Stonehouse 2008; HighScope 2018; NRC 2008). For example, the teacher and parents of an infant may decide together that they would like to encourage his independent exploration—out of the arms of the adult caregiver. They set a goal for both home and the child care setting of putting the baby on the floor with toys and the adult sitting next to him for support. As the baby learns to play contentedly by himself over time, the adult will gradually scoot farther and farther away.

It is important to plan to be responsive to individual infants and toddlers while also meeting the needs of the group. Plans arise naturally when teachers engage in continuous assessment, carefully organize and maintain children's records, and mindfully reflect on this information among themselves and with families.

Conclusion

Assessment in infant and toddler settings is a planned, everyday process based on strong positive relationships that are built on shared commitment among teachers, children, and families. Engaging in this process helps everyone work together to support the healthy development, learning, and well-being of infants and toddlers.

Reflection Questions

1. Multiple perspectives and ways of observing, including collaboration with families, often produce the most complete and accurate picture of each child. What are several ways that you already, or potentially could, gather information over time about each child's development and learning?

2. Developing strong, trusting relationships with families is essential to opening communication lines to share information about children and collaborating on goals to promote healthy growth, development, and learning. What are some ways that you build strong relationships with each family and promote two-way communication?

3. Describe some of the ways you capture and organize authentic observations of each child's growing competence in his everyday social environments.

4. What is one new approach to appropriate, meaningful, and family-centered child assessment described in this article that you would like to try?

5. In what ways do your current assessment practices emphasize the strengths of infants, toddlers, and families over their areas of need? What else can you do to increase the strengths-based focus of your child assessment practices?

References

CDE (California Department of Education). 2015. *Desired Results Developmental Profile: Infant/Toddler View.* Sacramento: CDE. www.desiredresults.us/sites/default/files/DRDP2015IT_091516.pdf.

Copple, C., & S. Bredekamp, eds. 2009. *Developmentally Appropriate Practice in Early Childhood Programs Serving Children from Birth Through Age 8.* 3rd ed. Washington, DC: NAEYC.

Dunst, C.J., M.B. Bruder, & M. Espe-Sherwindt. 2014. "Family Capacity-Building in Early Childhood Intervention: Do Context and Setting Matter?" *School Community Journal* 24 (1): 37–48.

Gestwicki, C. 2010. *Developmentally Appropriate Practice: Curriculum and Development in Early Education.* 4th ed. Belmont, CA: Wadsworth Cengage Learning.

Gonzalez-Mena, J., & A. Stonehouse. 2008. *Making Links: A Collaborative Approach to Planning and Practice in Early Childhood Programs.* New York: Teachers College Press.

HighScope. 2018. "Child Assessment." Accessed February 22. https://highscope.org/assessment/child.

Jarrett, M.H., B.C. Browne, & C.M. Wallin. 2006. "Using Portfolio Assessment to Document Developmental Progress of Infants and Toddlers." *Young Exceptional Children* 10 (1): 22–32.

Luckenbill, J. 2012. "Getting the Picture: Using the Digital Camera as a Tool to Support Reflective Practice and Responsive Care." *Young Children* 67 (2): 28–36.

Meisels, S., X. Wen, & K. Beachy-Quick. 2010. "Authentic Assessment for Infants and Toddlers: Exploring the Reliability and Validity of the Ounce Scale." *Applied Developmental Science* 14 (2): 55–71.

Moreno, A.J., & M.M. Klute. 2011. "Infant–Toddler Teachers Can Successfully Employ Authentic Assessment: The Learning Through Relating System." *Early Childhood Research Quarterly* 26 (4): 484–96.

NAEYC. 2003. "Early Childhood Curriculum, Assessment, and Program Evaluation: Building an Effective, Accountable System in Programs for Children Birth Through Age 8." Position statement with expanded resources. Washington, DC: NAEYC. www.naeyc.org/sites/default/files/globally-shared/downloads/PDFs/resources/position-statements/CAPEexpand.pdf.

NRC (National Research Council). 2008. *Early Childhood Assessment: Why, What, and How.* Washington, DC: National Academies Press. doi:10.17226/12446.

OHS (Office of Head Start). 2011. "Exploring the Essentials of Infant and Toddler Ongoing Assessment." Webcast.

ZERO TO THREE. 2010. *Infant/Toddler Development, Screening, and Assessment.* Washington, DC: ZERO TO THREE. www.zerotothree.org/resources/72-infant-and-toddler-development-screening-and-assessment.

About the Authors

James Elicker, PhD, is professor of human development and family studies at Purdue University. His research focuses on young children's development in the context of early childhood programs. He cofounded and codirected the Infant–Toddler Specialists of Indiana's professional development network and directed the Ben & Maxine Miller Child Development Laboratory School at Purdue University.

Mary Benson McMullen, PhD, is professor of early childhood education at Indiana University in Bloomington. Her current work focuses on indicators of quality and well-being in birth to 3 environments. She cofounded and codirects the Infant-Toddler Specialists of Indiana's professional development network.

Engaging Families in the Child Assessment Process

Margaret Caspe, Andrew Seltzer, Joy Lorenzo Kennedy, Moria Cappio, and Cristian DeLorenzo

A child's first assessors are her family. *Is she hungry? Does her diaper need to be changed? How is she growing?* When the young child enters an early childhood setting, though, the responsibility for developmental assessment is increasingly shared with teachers and other professionals. *Is she learning at an appropriate rate? Is she meeting her milestones? How can we tailor the program to better meet her strengths and needs?*

Because families play such an integral role in children's lives, it is essential for families and teachers to work together to promote children's development. For this reason, our organization, Children's Aid, has worked intentionally to make child assessment an integrated and collaborative effort between families and practitioners. This collaboration allows teachers and families to gain insight into a child's skills and developmental needs across the contexts of home, school, and community. Founded in 1853, Children's Aid currently provides early childhood services in New York City to more than 1,100 children from birth through age 5 and their families. We offer a variety of comprehensive home-based and center-based programs with an enriching curriculum, quality instruction, and a range of family supports that promote children's development, including family counseling and comprehensive health services.

Collaborative Assessment: Background and Definitions

Guidelines for administering and using child assessments emphasize the importance of involving families (NRC 2008). In the broadest sense, assessment refers to the ongoing process of monitoring a child's competencies and using this information to improve the child's learning (ECLKC 2017). Assessment often takes the form of teacher observation records, checklists that teachers complete, and samples of children's work. Involving families in this process enables them to share their expertise about their children and creates an exchange of information between families and teachers that supports children as their strengths and needs change.

Collaborative assessment creates a common basis for discussion, allowing teachers and families to set realistic goals for children's learning. Moreover, children thrive when they are part of a community in which families and teachers understand children's strengths and areas of need and then individualize teaching to match the children's capabilities (Copple & Bredekamp 2009). For example, a child might demonstrate emerging mathematical ability in the home when involved in routine activities like counting the number of dinner plates when setting the table. However, the child might have difficulty transferring those competencies to number activities in the classroom. Collaborative assessment shines a spotlight on these discontinuities to help teachers support the child's development.

Promising Practices for Engaging Families in the Assessment Process

While there is consensus that families should be involved in the assessment process, different branches of the early childhood field tend to conceptualize families' roles and responsibilities in overlapping yet different ways. Each branch contributes important lessons on the best ways to engage families in child assessment. Children's Aid has used a combination of these approaches with children in our programs from birth through age 5. At Children's Aid we attempt to draw from three perspectives (see "How Different Branches of the Early Education Field Integrate Families into the Assessment Process" on page 33) to develop strategies that better integrate families into our child assessment process. The following are five promising practices that our educational team has instituted to foster collaborative child assessment.

1. Create Various Opportunities for Families and Teachers to Communicate

Families and teachers need numerous opportunities to communicate about children's development (Lawrence-Lightfoot 2004; McWilliams & Patton 2015). To be meaningful, the information teachers provide to families must be unbiased, clear, jargon free, and presented in different ways. Some families prefer seeing charts and checklists of children's progress, while others prefer portfolios or observational narratives. It is important for educators to provide notes and documentation in each family's home language.

While family–teacher conferences are one important avenue for conversations about children's progress, ongoing written notes, phone calls, and home visits also offer occasions for parents and teachers to discuss an individual child's assessments. In each of these

How Different Branches of the Early Education Field Integrate Families into the Assessment Process

Role	Focus	Mechanisms
Psychologists and special needs experts	Using family-centered assessment	■ Putting families at the center of the assessment process ■ Promoting families as informants, raters of child behavior, and/or active assessors (Crais, Roy, & Free 2006)
Early childhood practitioners	Fostering family engagement	■ Employing effective observational tools and techniques in the classroom ■ Creating effective family–practitioner interactions ■ Integrating families' input and assessment measures into the existing structure of the teaching day (Jablon, Dombro, & Dichtelmiller 2007)
Early childhood advocates and policy makers	Empowering families	■ Providing families with access to assessment information and data ■ Supporting families' understanding of the information provided ■ Creating opportunities for families to take action on behalf of their children, based on assessment results (HFRP 2013)

interactions, it is important to find ways for families to receive the information *and* take an active role in the assessment process. To achieve this, Children's Aid programs use both formal standardized tools and organic informal discussions.

For instance, our Early Head Start programs use The Ounce Scale assessment for children ages 0–36 months, which contains a Family Album component (Meisels et al. 2003). Parents receive a booklet in which to write down, draw, or include photos to show their own observations of their children. They use these to prompt conversations with teachers. Although families complete this activity as part of a standardized assessment, teachers in other programs can easily draw on scrapbooking and journaling as ways for families to chronicle children's development in the home and share their observations with the children's teachers.

Children's Aid early childhood programs also use the Ages & Stages Questionnaires, third edition (ASQ-3), for children ages 0–5, in which both families and teachers rate children on various aspects of their development (Squires & Bricker 2009). In our 0–3 programs, home visitors complete the questionnaires together with families. In our preschool-age programs, families answer the questionnaires at home and return them to the teachers, who review the results and use them as a starting point for discussion. Both methods allow our staff to gain the family's perspectives on the child and her social, emotional, and cognitive development, and to ensure that communication is bi-directional, with information flowing in both directions between families and practitioners.

Our programs also rely on informal discussions to understand families' evaluations of their children. For example, a mother recently approached a Children's Aid teacher with concerns that her child was extremely active at home. She was worried that he might have an attention disorder. The teacher, however, did not observe these behaviors in the classroom. After consulting with the program psychologist (one of this article's authors), the teacher invited the mother to observe the child in the classroom. The clinician joined the observation, and while the two watched the child, he explained the different ways he perceived the child showing control and attentive mastery of his environment. This guided observation helped alleviate the mother's concerns and gave the teacher deeper insight into how the structure of her classroom was benefiting the child's development.

2. Ensure Assessments Include Children's Development and Behavior in Multiple Settings

Children develop and learn in multiple settings, including the home environment, the early education setting, the neighborhood, and the larger culture (Bronfenbrenner 1989). A complete assessment evaluates how children perform at the program and at home. In Children's Aid programs, our family advocates begin the enrollment process by conducting a home visit, during which they get to know the family and child by interviewing them at home. Although the home visits are made as part of the Early Head Start and Head Start requirements, this method is an extraordinary way for any practitioner to develop trusting relationships with families and gain better insight into children's development as well as their social and cultural backgrounds. Even short 30-minute visits make a difference.

Shortly after visiting the home, family advocates conduct a Family Partnership Assessment (FPA) either in the home or at the program. The FPA is an approximately 40-item questionnaire developed by Children's Aid staff that taps into the seven family outcomes promoted in the Head Start Parent, Family, and Community Engagement Framework (HHS 2011), such as family well-being and positive parent–child relationships. Staff ask families to speak about their daily life in the home, their community participation, their interactions with each other and their children, their perceptions of their children, and their hopes and dreams for themselves and their children. For instance, families indicate how often they read books at home, visit the library, or sing songs with their children—all behaviors that are highly predictive of children's success in school. Moreover, families specify different workshop topics they are interested in or ways they might need support for their well-being. This process is particularly important for Children's Aid programs because we serve a predominantly immigrant population who might not be familiar with the US education system. The FPA provides an opportunity for us to begin a conversation with families regarding their strengths and about program and school expectations.

In addition, staff from different program areas (for example, special needs coordinator, mental health workers, health clinicians, classroom teachers, and home visitors) come together at least once a year (or more frequently depending on a family's needs) to meet in coordinated conferences to share their perspectives on each child. This integrated approach generates an understanding of a child and his family, and allows staff to formulate strategies that include the entire family when seeking the best way to assist the child. Understanding the family context also allows staff to connect families with the comprehensive supports they need.

3. Use Assessment Results to Connect Home and School Teaching Practices

Assessment results provide teachers and families with greater understanding of children's development. However, it is not enough for family members to understand their children's development. Families must have the tools, resources, and confidence to act on this information to further children's learning in supportive and caring relationships (HFRP 2013). As one example, in response to evaluation findings showing that the language and literacy development of children in Children's Aid programs needed more attention, teachers and families worked together to create developmentally and culturally appropriate home–school connection activities for families and children to do at home.

When developing the activities for preschool-age children, we learned that many families supported children's language and literacy in the home by sharing elaborate oral stories—detailed narratives told with vivid vocabulary about true or imaginary events—with their children, rather than reading books with them. To build on this family strength, we took photographs of the surrounding community and developed questions to match each picture, with the intent to spark new and interesting conversations between families and children. For example, we provided a photograph of an ambulance in one of the activities, asking, "Why do you think an ambulance makes such a loud noise?" and "Where does an ambulance travel?" Activities can also be tailored to the specific needs of each child. For example, with children for whom letter, number, shape, or color recognition is a targeted growth area, families might also choose to talk about the letters and words on the ambulance or the colors they see.

As part of the language and literacy development project, once a month preschool teachers ask families to reflect informally on using the activities, noting their thoughts in a journal. These journal reflections provide an important window into families' assessments of their children's learning. We learned that families using these activities see many changes in their 3- and 4-year-old children over the course of the year in different developmental areas.

Families report being surprised by what their children say during activities, indicate that they didn't realize that their children knew certain things, and are proud of their children's abilities to explain books, count, or sing. These activities bolster the parent–child relationship, help families increase the ways they use language and learning opportunities during daily routines, and encourage families to set aside specific time to listen to children share their feelings and ideas.

4. Help Families Make Connections Between Assessments and Educational Standards

Early childhood practitioners are increasingly called on to align curriculum and instruction with standards developed at the local, state, and national levels (NAEYC 2012). These standards are critical in helping teachers and families understand the generally agreed-on developmental expectations for children of different ages. For example, early childhood professionals throughout New York follow the New York State Prekindergarten Foundation for the Common Core, which indicate that children in prekindergarten are expected to demonstrate increasing awareness and competence in several areas, including physical development and health, social and emotional development, and language and literacy (NYSED 2011).

Today, a variety of assessment systems that align with these prekindergarten standards are available for teacher use; two such examples are the Work Sampling System and Teaching Strategies GOLD. Children's Aid uses one of these assessment systems, and preschool teachers have reported that it provides an effective starting point for conversations with families about setting goals for children's learning. For example, systems provide parent–teacher conference forms and online parent newsletter templates that concretely link children's progress to expectations for typical developmental progression.

In addition, we have found that classroom meetings, parenting groups, schoolwide workshops, and in-school family events provide a chance for preschool staff and families to talk about standards and how they relate to child development and learning milestones. During these discussions, practitioners and families can explore what children should know and be able to do at different ages, and how the prevailing standards might differ from expectations when the parents were growing up. These conversations are especially important for families who might have been educated in different countries and are new to the school system in the United States. Moreover, by aggregating child-level assessment data—that is, by mathematically combining data about groups of children to provide an overall summary of their progress—practitioners can talk to families about overall program performance. Using assessment results in this way allows families to understand how their individual child compares to others of the same age both at the local program level and in comparison to national norms. We also explain that each child follows an individual path for development in the early years and that development can be uneven across domains. For example, a child might excel in gross motor skills in comparison to her peers but need additional supports in social and emotional development.

5. Invite Families to Join a Community of Learners Around Child Assessment

To effectively engage families in collaborative assessment, it is important that all stakeholders in the process come together to share ideas and lessons learned. This can happen at the program and community levels. As an example of community-level engagement, in 2011 and again in 2012, a group of local parents, practitioners, researchers, policy makers, and advocates convened at New York University's Forum on Children and Families to discuss child assessment (CFPC 2012). Following the 2011 Forum, a working group explored family engagement in the assessment process. The group created a Parents' Bill of Rights designed to better inform parents about their rights during the child assessment process; this bill of rights was then presented and disseminated at the 2012 Forum. The bill of rights included items such as

› The right for families to be treated with respect and to be a part of the assessment process

› The right to request a meeting with program staff who can explain the child's assessment results in a language families can understand

Children's Aid administrators participated in this community-wide effort to foster a collaborative relationship between teachers and families throughout the assessment process and circulated information back to teachers and families at program sites.

In addition to these kinds of community-level opportunities, at the program level our early childhood administrators bring teachers together regularly throughout the year to discuss classroom-based assessments. For example, at the beginning of every year, formal training

Culturally and Linguistically Appropriate Assessment

The children and families who participate in Children's Aid early childhood programs are culturally, linguistically, and socioeconomically diverse. Nearly 48 percent are Latino, 32 percent are African American or African, and 20 percent are another heritage. Almost 60 percent of the children served have parents born outside of the United States, with nearly 48 percent entering our programs speaking Spanish, French, and African languages. At least 84 percent live at or below the poverty line. A central tenet of our work around assessment is that all families have important information to share with us about their children and our program. We believe it is our responsibility to develop trusting relationships with families and to design opportunities so that families feel safe having open, honest conversations with us.

We do this in many ways. First, we seek to learn about and support the ways families talk, play, and engage with their children at home and in their community. This gives us insight into the types of assessment situations that children will be comfortable with. It also helps us work with families to choose instruments that are linguistically and culturally appropriate. Using family scrapbooks to monitor and gauge our youngest children's development is an invaluable way for families to meaningfully and authentically participate in the assessment process. We also take care to assess children across all of the settings in which they learn. Children learn everywhere, all the time—at home, in the classroom, in the library, or at the park. By engaging families in the assessment process, we are better able to understand how children learn and grow in these multiple contexts. Finally, we work with families to assess children across time. Assessment is not a one-time event, and we invite each family to frequently reflect on how their child changes, what new skills she develops, and how her understanding of the world evolves.

is conducted for all Children's Aid home visitors of children ages 0–3 and teachers of 3- and 4-year-olds to ensure that they are administering and scoring mandatory screening assessments in the correct way across all programs. We also bring the teachers together to review as a group children's work samples to ensure that the teachers understand and rate children's abilities consistently. It is essential that the teachers all use the different scoring rubrics in the same manner, so families can be sure that, for example, a *4* means the same thing from one classroom to the next. This gives families confidence that the assessment process is objective and that their children would be assessed the same way by a teacher in another class.

We are now beginning to include families in these trainings and discussions. While this is a new area of focus, we believe that it will help us improve in our attempts to understand, respect, and incorporate families' cultural backgrounds into our assessment practices. Some steps we hope to take to improve these efforts are to (1) conduct informal interviews with a diverse group of families to see how they assess children's work and understand their perspectives, and (2) invite groups of families to talk to teachers about their own methods of evaluating their children's growth in the home.

Conclusion

Effective child assessment integrates families into the assessment process in a collaborative and welcoming exchange of knowledge. The suggestions we provide here are methods that Children's Aid programs have used to foster successful collaborative assessment. An integrated, collaborative assessment approach creates many opportunities for two-way communication, empowers families, and takes both cultural differences and formal standards into account, all within a community of learners. Families are the constant in children's lives: they are the experts on their children's habits, interests, and abilities. By inviting families to participate in the assessment process, early childhood educators gain access to an invaluable resource for understanding each child's individual needs and abilities.

Reflection Questions

1. How does your program engage families in the assessment process?

2. Reflect on when and how you inform and include families in the assessment process. After reading this article, are there any new approaches you would like to try?

3. How do you make assessment data accessible to families?

4. What opportunities do you provide for families to understand and make sense of the assessment data?

5. Reflect on how you develop practical tips and ideas for families to do together with their children based on assessment data you've collected. How might you include families in generating these ideas?

References

Bronfenbrenner, U. 1989. "Ecological Systems Theory." *Annals of Child Development* 6: 187–249.

CFPC (Child & Family Policy Center). 2012. "Improving Child-Level Assessments in Early Childhood Educational Settings." Policy brief. *Forum on Children and Families,* Issue 3. New York: CFPC. http://steinhardt.nyu.edu/scmsAdmin/media/users/lec321/ForumBrief_FINAL_2.15.13.pdf.

Copple, C., & S. Bredekamp, eds. 2009. *Developmentally Appropriate Practice in Early Childhood Programs Serving Children from Birth Through Age 8*. 3rd ed. Washington, DC: NAEYC.

Crais, E.R., V.P. Roy, & K. Free. 2006. "Parents' and Professionals' Perceptions of the Implementation of Family-Centered Practices in Child Assessments." *American Journal of Speech-Language Pathology* 15 (4): 365–77.

ECLKC (Early Childhood Learning and Knowledge Center). 2017. "Learning From Assessment (LFA) Toolkit." Last modified October 31. https://eclkc.ohs.acf.hhs.gov/child-screening-assessment/learning-assessment-lfa-toolkit/learning-assessment-lfa-toolkit.

HFRP (Harvard Family Research Project). 2013. *Tips for Administrators, Teachers, and Families: How to Share Data Effectively*. Cambridge, MA: HFRP. https://globalfrp.org/Articles/Tips-for-Administrators-Teachers-and-Families-How-to-Share-Data-Effectively.

HHS (US Department of Health and Human Services). 2011. *The Head Start Parent, Family, and Community Engagement Framework: Promoting Family Engagement and School Readiness From Prenatal to Age 8*. Washington, DC: HHS. https://eclkc.ohs.acf.hhs.gov/pdguide/media/resource_files/PFCEFramework.pdf

Jablon, J.R., A.L. Dombro, & M.L. Dichtelmiller. 2007. *The Power of Observation*. 2nd ed. Washington, DC: Teaching Strategies.

Lawrence-Lightfoot, S. 2004. *The Essential Conversation: What Parents and Teachers Can Learn From Each Other*. New York: Ballantine.

McWilliams, L., & C. Patton. 2015. "How to Share Data with Families." *Educational Leadership* 73 (3): 46–49.

Meisels, S.J., D.B. Marsden, A.L. Dombro, D.R. Weston, & A.M. Jewkes. 2003. *The Ounce Scale: An Observational Assessment for Infants, Toddlers, and Families*. New York: Pearson Early Learning.

NAEYC. 2012. *The Common Core State Standards: Caution and Opportunity for Early Childhood Education*. Washington, DC: NAEYC. www.naeyc.org/sites/default/files/globally-shared/downloads/PDFs/resources/topics/11_commoncore1_2a_rv2.pdf.

NRC (National Research Council). 2008. *Early Childhood Assessment: Why, What, and How*. Washington, DC: National Academies Press. doi:10.17226/12446.

NYSED (New York State Education Department). 2011. *The New York State Prekindergarten Foundation for the Common Core*. New York: NYSED. www.p12.nysed.gov/ciai/common_core_standards/pdfdocs/nyslsprek.pdf.

Squires, J., & D. Bricker. 2009. *Ages & Stages Questionnaires*. 3rd ed. Baltimore: Brookes Publishing.

About the Authors

Margaret Caspe, PhD, is director of research and professional learning at Global Family Research Project. She focuses on the role of family engagement in supporting children's learning.

Andrew Seltzer, EdD, is deputy director of family services at Children's Aid in New York City.

Joy Lorenzo Kennedy, PhD, is the scientific support specialist for Databrary, a web-based platform for sharing developmental research.

Moria Cappio, EdM, is vice president of early childhood programs at Children's Aid.

Cristian DeLorenzo, MS, is senior director of program design and management at Shine Early Learning, a division of Acelero Learning.

Photographs: pp. 31, 35, © Getty Images

Using Observation to Build STEAM Experiences

Angela Eckhoff and Sandra M. Linder

During the first weeks of school, life can be chaotic for preschool teachers. We're busy organizing the classroom, establishing routines, and setting shared expectations with children. It can be hard to find time to observe children during the day. But short observation periods are critical opportunities for teachers to learn about children, and the new year is an excellent time to make sure observing children becomes part of your daily work as a teacher. Noticing where children choose to play, which peers they interact with, and how they explore the classroom gives teachers a deeper understanding of children's interests, knowledge, and skills. These interests can guide STEAM (science, technology, engineering, art, and mathematics) investigations throughout the year. While classroom projects should be fun and creative, and offer opportunities for in-depth learning, it's essential that they be grounded in children's interests and curiosity.

Observation in Everyday Experiences

Observation enables you to identify the areas where children are just beginning to grasp concepts—like making a plan to solve a problem that comes up during play—and where they have a solid foundation—such as making careful observations and predictions. Teachers can use classroom observations to assess children's levels of understanding informally as children engage in their regular classrooms activities and routines. When teachers consistently observe children, they get to know a great deal about them. This knowledge enhances teacher–child interactions and comes in handy during lesson planning, as you can see in Mr. Dinh's classroom.

Mr. Dinh sees a group of children in the dramatic play area struggling to negotiate who sets the table, how to divide up the food they cooked, and where they should sit as they play together. As he observes, Mr. Dinh learns which children take charge in pretend play, which children are more verbal in their interactions, how long it is before individual children become frustrated, and what directions their curiosity and imaginations take. Mr. Dinh uses what he learns to introduce a STEAM-based investigation into the day.

Before snack time, he talks with this group about his observations: "I noticed when you were playing that you were cooking and getting ready to eat a meal. Tell me about how you set the table and served the food. Did you have any problems?"

The children explain that there were not enough plates for each person at the table to have one. As they describe the situation, they focus on the idea of fairness: "There were five of us in the house but only three plates in the cupboard. It wasn't fair that Lilly and Stone didn't have plates."

After listening to and commenting on the children's answers, Mr. Dinh presents a problem related to the children's struggles. They must work together to solve it as a group. "Today, instead of having individual snacks, I have a bag of pretzels, two bowls, two scoops, and a pile of paper plates. How can we work together to make sure everyone at the two tables has the same number of pretzels? And can we do it without touching other people's food with our fingers?"

The children discuss ideas, and together they decide on a strategy for distributing the plates and pretzels to the group. After the snack is passed out, Mr. Dinh leads a conversation about the steps the children took to carry out the task and resolve difficulties: "First, we counted the number of people at each table, then we counted out the number of plates. Next, we gave one plate to each person. We poured pretzels into each of the two big bowls and we passed a bowl with a scoop around each table so everyone could serve themselves using the scoop. Then we combined the extra pretzels in a bowl and passed it around the room. Each person could take one more pretzel until there were none left."

What Makes this a STEAM Investigation?

STEAM investigations are inquiry-based learning experiences in science, technology, engineering, art, and mathematics. Children actively work with a variety of materials to explore, experiment, question, problem solve, and create. Teachers act as guides and facilitators to support children as they work, encouraging them to think about what they're experiencing.

While extensive planning is sometimes required, STEAM investigations can at times evolve naturally from everyday situations. In the vignette above, Mr. Dinh used snack time for an

investigation based on his observations of the children's play, focusing on processes of inquiry from STEAM, including asking questions, reasoning, communicating, collaborating, and representing ideas in a variety of ways.

Meaningful STEAM investigations can begin with a problem or challenge children encounter. The teacher provides an opportunity for the children to investigate and collaborate with each other to develop a plan to solve the problem. While the snack challenge had clear connections to math content (counting, measuring), the main issue was to develop a plan for distributing the plates and pretzels equally—without touching one another's food.

Designing STEAM Provocations

In addition to creating STEAM activities from children's everyday experiences, teachers can develop and implement open-ended explorations—also known as *provocations*. The concept of provocations comes from the Reggio Emilia philosophy. It describes activities that don't have a preordained outcome or specific objective. Instead, provocations encourage children to explore freely and dive into new actions, ideas, and ways of thinking.

Provocation activities can take place in the learning centers of your classroom or outdoors in a play space, and children can work individually, with partners, or in small groups. To set up provocations, carefully select materials related to the topic you are exploring (for example, gears, nuts and bolts, scraps of wood, and other building materials for engineering provocations). Rather than give specific directions for using the materials, let the children explore and investigate the materials in their own way. Include documentation materials, like markers, pencils, crayons, clay, digital cameras, and paper, that the children (and you) can use as they investigate the materials. Choose activities that require children to use thinking and planning skills, promoting creativity.

Supporting Children with Delays or Disabilities

As you plan your STEAM observations, think about the unique needs of children with delays or disabilities in your classroom. When observing a child with a disability at play, be sure to look at how he engages in the activity with his usual adaptations or supports. If a child usually uses a communication device when playing with his peers, observe at a time when he has this device readily available.

Observing when typical supports are not in place will give you an inaccurate picture of the child's understanding. You may need to observe a child with a delay or disability more often, and in a greater variety of situations, than you typically do before you can gather enough information about his knowledge and interests to design meaningful learning experiences.

Provocations provide opportunities for more intentional observations. For example, if you are interested in learning what children know and understand about natural materials, you might create a provocation area where children engage with a variety of rocks, sticks, leaves, sand, seashells, cotton, and other materials.

Pay close attention to what interests the children, the conversations they have, and the questions they ask. Use that information to deepen their learning and plan future activities. For instance, if children pay particular attention to the differences in the appearance of rocks, you might decide to develop a series of earth science explorations or create a science center dedicated to studying rocks.

Organizing STEAM Observations

Choose a method of observation that will allow you to best understand what the children know and what they are working to understand. For example, to understand what they know about quantity, observe them while they build with blocks, which encourages the use of mathematics language (more, less, greater, fewer, same, and equal).

Be consistent and intentional in your observations, and reserve time every day to observe. A checklist of key skills and language is a useful guide and helps keep your observations focused and on track. Intentional observation and careful reflection can help you identify and understand the reasons behind children's behaviors and actions, especially with children who have challenging behavior. In turn, this will help you implement strategies like modifying the environment or acknowledging and reinforcing appropriate behaviors (Brillante 2017).

Be sure to observe all of the children. Take notes and review them at the end of each week to ensure that you aren't leaving anyone out. If you have more than one teacher in your room, assign each teacher specific children to observe to ensure that every child is observed regularly.

Here are suggestions for making use of your observation notes, photographs, and videos of the children's explorations:

> **Identify** areas of, or ideas related to, children's interests. Discuss them with other teachers to support curriculum development across subject areas—such as music and movement, science, and social studies.

> **Develop** lessons that directly build on children's ideas captured during observation.

> **Modify** the materials or centers children have engaged with to further support their explorations.

> **Create** classroom or individual documentation using your notes, photographs, video, and children's work samples. Observation notes can be included in many types of documentation, including portfolios, bulletin boards, and documentation panels.

Conclusion

Observations offer starting points for developing meaningful learning experiences that build on children's knowledge and interests and help you build a STEAM-oriented classroom environment. Problem-solving experiences should be authentic so children can make connections between their own experiences and problems presented to them.

Reflection Questions

1. Think about your daily classroom schedule and routines. Identify a few opportunities when you could regularly observe children's play.

2. As you watch children play, note which experiences interest or excite them most. How might you use that curiosity to create a meaningful STEAM investigation?

3. Set up a provocation activity, and as children explore and experiment with the materials, consider the following:

   a. What questions are they asking each other?

   b. Which experiences do they handle with confidence?

   c. In which experiences do they seem to be more hesitant, struggle, or have misunderstandings?

4. Based on your observation notes, what next steps could you take to extend children's STEAM learning? For example, do children need more time or repeated experiences with a topic to build their confidence and make connections among the ideas they generate through their discoveries?

5. Is there a learning center in your classroom that children no longer use or rarely show interest in? What kind of modifications could you make to reignite their interest?

Reference

Brillante, P. 2017. *The Essentials: Supporting Young Children with Disabilities in the Classroom.* Washington, DC: NAEYC.

About the Authors

Angela Eckhoff is associate professor of teaching and learning in the early childhood education program at Old Dominion University, in Norfolk, Virginia. She is coeditor of *Young Children's* Growing in STEM column and *Teaching Young Children's* Full STEAM Ahead column.

Sandra M. Linder is associate professor of early childhood mathematics education at Clemson University, in Clemson, South Carolina. She is coeditor of *Young Children's* Growing in STEM column and *Teaching Young Children's* Full STEAM Ahead column.

Photographs: p. 40, © Julia Luckenbill; p. 42, © Vera Wiest

Learning Stories

Judi Pack

When I first read about New Zealand's Learning Stories approach, I was most impressed with its potential for connecting with families by sharing with them the awesomeness of their children while making visible the power of play.

The Learning Stories Assessment approach is a form of observation and documentation that is written in a narrative story format (Carr & Lee 2012). The teacher watches and listens as children explore through play. She may take a photo or two, jot down some notes, and create a story about what she has seen to share with children and their families.

A story is powerful and meaningful to families of preschoolers and can often communicate more than a number, a score, or a checklist of skills. Because the story is written *to* the children, it's both easy for teachers to write and easy for families to understand. Teachers become observers and story writers while reflecting on children's actions and words. The story is always a positive one about children's strengths, good ideas, and dispositions for learning.

I like to think of it as observing small moments that provide big opportunities.

Creating a Learning Story

› **Write the story.** Describe what the child did and said, then provide your perspective on it. Add a title.

› **Read the story to the child.** Listen for her comments and feedback. You can also read the story to the entire group of children as long as the child in the story agrees to share it. Sharing a story can sometimes spark ideas for other children.

› **Plan.** Describe what you will do to enhance or extend the play. This is an opportunity to reflect on the child's play while planning for a group of children or one child. Will you add more or different materials? Provide books for research or books for story reading?

› **Connect to families.** Give a copy of the story to the family, along with a note asking for their feedback. The note might say, "This is a story about your child. I would appreciate any feedback or comments you wish to share."

You can share more information about what the child has learned or is learning and attach that to the story when you place it in the child's portfolio.

What to Look for When Documenting a Learning Story

› **Child-initiated play.** The play comes from the child's ideas, interests, or discoveries.

› **Engagement.** The child is deeply engaged and sustains the play or inquiry for some time.

› **Intentionality.** The child has a plan or goal in mind.

› **Relationships.** The child is engaged with others or with materials in a way that is new, unusual, or insightful to the teacher, which could help the teacher determine the focus of the learning story.

› **Learning disposition.** The child's way of learning—or his approach to figuring things out—is revealed.

Benefits of Learning Stories

Learning stories benefit children, teachers, families, and the entire program and community.

For children. As you listen to, observe, and record children's explorations, they see that you value their ideas and thinking. Hearing their stories offers valuable opportunities for children to reflect on their own thinking and learning and to share their ideas about each other's stories when they are shared in a group.

For teachers. Carefully observing children at play and reflecting on these observations gives teachers knowledge about individual children over time, and stories capture the moments in each child's daily life that will create a comprehensive profile of the child. Through the process of creating and

An Example of a Simple Learning Story

The Story: How Agnes Scooped the Sand

To Agnes—

It was interesting to watch you scoop up and experiment with the sand. You were learning about its qualities and concentrated for a long time to do what you wanted to do. It looked frustrating because there was so little sand, but that did not stop you. Your work was slow and steady. Sometimes other children got in your way or interrupted, but you just kept on going! It was so much fun to watch you at work.

I think you were deciding a lot of things, including which tools to use and how you should use them. You were thinking about what you should use to make the sand scooping work best. You used a small scoop and then a detergent top. You were learning about learning!

To be a good learner, you have to stick with things and spend time on them. You did that!

What Next?

Tomorrow, I will add more sand to the pool so that the sand scooping will not be so frustrating and the results will be more satisfying. I will also add more scoops and tools and, perhaps, place a bucket of water nearby to invite further exploration. I'm going to look for a book about sandcastles and playing at the beach. This might interest Agnes and other children since it is almost summertime and some families may be heading to the beach. And, of course, a good book will help expand on their growing vocabulary and language around this type of play.

Attach a sheet that families can return to you:

Hello! I have enclosed Agnes's latest learning story. What do you think?

What We Learned About Agnes

As Agnes played with the sand, she learned about the qualities and quirkiness of sand—how it flows, sticks, and feels on the skin. This is real science at work! She developed a variety of strategies in deciding which tools to use and mathematical thinking in choosing the container size, comparing containers, and estimating which would work best. She used her fine and gross motor skills, especially hand–eye coordination, which will help her as she begins writing. Most important, Agnes went about her task with confidence, curiosity, and persistence. All of these are qualities that are needed for deep learning.

sharing stories, teachers learn more about their group of children, child development in general, and how children learn. Rather than planning learning opportunities that originate from outside the child's own perspective and understanding, teachers use stories and other documentation to develop appropriate, meaningful curriculum and interactions that address children's interests and needs.

For families and teacher–family relationships. To families, learning stories illustrate how much the teacher values their children, how she plans for their learning, and that she herself is a thoughtful, continual learner. Providing information about children's strengths in a friendly, authentic format that illustrates how children learn through play opens the door for continuing conversations with families and encourages families to share their input. It is also a vehicle to help families and children share and talk about children's school experiences. Stories spotlight the ways children are natural learners, eager investigators, and capable problem solvers.

For the program. Stories can be used to broadcast the strengths and capabilities of children to families and others in the program and wider community. Using learning stories as discussion prompts at staff meetings and for staff collaboration—along with creating books, displays, or slides for families, children, and other teachers—are some of the ways children's knowledge and skills can be shared with others.

Supporting Dual Language Learners

The Learning Stories Assessment approach is a wonderful technique for connecting with children who are growing up learning two or more languages, known as dual language learners (DLLs). While a teacher may not speak or understand a DLL's home language, she can observe his learning, perceptions, and capabilities in action as the child plays. For instance, children may construct dramatic play scenarios that are replications of their home life experiences, opening a window into their culture and customs that the teacher can both learn from and appreciate.

Because learning stories help bridge a child's home and the program, it is worth the effort to have the story written in the family's home language. Consider inviting bilingual volunteers to help you write and translate learning stories in the children's home languages. Be sure to share this article with the volunteers so they can understand the significance of this valuable interaction.

Reflection Questions

1. How can you plan time to write at least one learning story each day?

2. In what ways might you and your colleagues collaborate and support each other through sharing learning stories?

3. What other benefits do you think this approach has for children?

4. How might you share a learning story with children and their families in their home language if you do not speak it?

5. When you share a child's learning story with her family, how could you encourage the family to reply or give feedback?

The Dispositions for Learning that Teachers Need

For teachers to embrace learning stories, they

> Are curious about how children learn and think

> Regard children's ideas as worthwhile and interesting

> Believe in the importance of connecting with parents in meaningful ways

> Are self-reflective and willing to use the stories as a catalyst for further understanding, growth, and action

Conclusion

Learning stories can respectfully connect teachers with families and build strong relationships. When they write stories, teachers become better observers of children and develop their storytelling voice to joyfully share with the entire community.

Reference

Carr, M., & W. Lee. 2012. *Learning Stories: Constructing Learner Identities in Early Education*. London, UK: SAGE Publications.

About the Author

Judi Pack works as an independent consultant. She encourages early childhood professionals to listen carefully to children in order to build on their ideas and interests and focus on the joy of being together, discovering, and learning.

Photographs: pp. 45, 46, 47, 48, courtesy of the author

The Power of Documentation in the Early Childhood Classroom

Hilary Seitz

A parent notices something on the wall in the hallway near her child's classroom. She stops and looks across the entire wall, as if trying to determine where to start. She moves to the left a bit and scans the bulletin board posted farther down. At one point she nods as if in agreement and mouths a yes. Another parent approaches and turns to see what is on the wall. He too is mesmerized by the documentation of what one child discovered about pussy willows by using an i-Scope lens.

What Is Documentation?

Documentation is the process of carefully observing children, collecting artifacts (such as work samples, photos, and comments from children on their work) about the observation, and then displaying these items for an audience. Documentation can focus on individual or group experiences, activities, and learning. When the teacher uses this in-depth form of documentation as a process and a tool for learning rather than simply as a display, Stacey (2015) refers to it as *pedagogical documentation*.

Effective Communication

An effective piece of documentation tells the story and the purpose of an event, experience, or development. It is a product that draws others into the experience—evidence or artifacts that describe a situation, tell a story, and help the viewer to understand the purpose of the action.

When used effectively, consistently, and thoughtfully, documentation can also drive curriculum and collaboration in preschool and kindergarten classrooms.

Formats that Work

A bulletin board can be a form of documentation, but there are any number of other possible formats, including a presentation board containing documentation artifacts and/or evidence (documentation panels), class books, ePortfolios, websites, or other social media platforms.

The format that documentation takes can be as varied as the creator's mind permits. Because documentation should provide evidence of a process with a purpose, whatever the format, it should fully explain the process, highlighting various aspects of the experience or event.

Audience and Purposes

Successful documentation formats reflect the intended audience and purposes. In addition, the format selected will depend on the individual preparing the documentation and how the children are involved in the experience.

For example, if one teacher wants to highlight for families and administrators how the class is meeting a particular math or science standard, she would use examples of children participating in experiences that align with the standard. As evidence, she might include photographs of children measuring plant stems with a ruler, children's comments about measuring the stems, background information about how the children learned about measurement (or plants), and the specific learning standard the children are meeting by participating in this experience. To best combine all of these elements, the teacher may choose a physical documentation panel or a website that is updated regularly as the format to help the audience understand how children are learning.

If children in the class are the intended audience, however, and the purpose of the documentation is to help children reflect on their math and science learning and connect them to future lessons, then the teacher would select different artifacts and evidence. A documentation panel or an interactive electronic bulletin board such as VoiceThread or

Documentation Artifacts and Evidence

› Teacher's description and overview of an event/experience/skill development, such as photographs and narratives of a field trip

› Photographs of children at work—for example, conducting a science experiment

› Samples of children's work, like a writing sample from the beginning of the year

› Children's comments, such as "All the rocks have sparkles in them," in writing or as recorded by the teacher

› Teacher or parent comments about a classroom event—for instance, "It was really fun helping the children measure the ingredients for playdough"

› Teacher transcriptions of conversations during small group time when children are exploring a new topic, such as why snow melts indoors

› Important items or observations relating to an event/experience/development, such as "Elijah can now write his own name on his work"

Possible Topics to Document

> Individual child growth and development, such as language development progression

> Expected behaviors (at group time, in using a certain toy, while eating together)

> Curriculum ideas or events (field trips, presentations, special activities, celebrations)

> Curriculum projects, such as learning about plant life cycles

> Families and relationships (different types of family structures and characteristics of the families in the classroom community)

> Evidence of meeting learning standards (by posting work samples)

> Questions and answers from children, teachers, and families about topics like classroom routines, such as how to wash your hands

---

Glogster may be appropriate, but different artifacts and evidence might include a web of children's ideas—for instance, why an elephant should not live at the Alaska Zoo, children's comments about the elephant, and questions for further exploration, such as "Where should an elephant live?" Related photographs and work samples might be added.

Again, an explanation about where the learning began and where it is intended to go will help any audience better understand the documentation. In both cases, the quality of the end product will depend on the teacher's understanding of the children, the curriculum, and the standards, along with her effective use of technology and observation.

What Should You Document?

A variety of experiences and topics are appropriate to document, but documentation should always tell a complete story. To stay on track, carefully select one topic and explore it to the fullest rather than trying to do a little of everything. For example, if the class is learning about plants (studying plant parts, how to grow particular plants, types of plants, and so on), it would be best to document fully just one aspect of the learning.

Choosing a Focus

The teacher might choose to document only the children's study of plant parts, for example, and could start by providing a learning spark, such as a new plant in the classroom (Seitz 2006). As children comment on the plant parts, the teacher can create a web to record what they know and to help them formulate questions. The children might also draw and label the various plant parts.

Presenting the Topic and Learning

The teacher can combine all of these pieces to make a documentation panel or online display through a website or social media platform. This documentation would illustrate the children's knowledge and understanding more thoroughly than a panel displaying every child's watercolor paintings of a plant and every brainstormed list of vegetable plants. Offering specific examples of how children came to their understandings about just one aspect of a lesson—in this case, plant parts—achieves more than offering an overview of several experiences.

Showing Developmental Progress

One important and common topic for documentation is individual child growth and development. As previous examples have shown, the documenter is a researcher first, collecting as much information as possible to paint a picture of progress and outcomes. Documenting individual growth requires a great deal of research, as the teacher must observe each child in a variety of areas of development (such as social and emotional, cognitive, language, and motor) over a substantial length of time. Only then can the teacher create a documentation piece that tells an accurate story about each child.

A teacher should be careful to avoid displaying private or confidential information in public forums like a public Facebook group. There are times when documentation may be more appropriately shared in other, more private venues, such as an ePortfolio. The ePortfolio could show individual growth, progress, and learning as well as examples of how the child collaborates in the classroom community.

Portfolios used for individual assessment of children make a particularly good format for documenting developmental progress. Teachers select several domains to research. They then collect evidence of a child's interaction with other children (photographs and written observations), record the child's reflections about their friendships and cognitive abilities in interviews or group discussions, collect work samples, and tie the documentation together by writing a narrative describing the child's abilities (not deficits) in the selected domains. Even though the portfolio focuses on a child's abilities, teachers may want to consider sharing the documentation or portfolio in a private setting, such as at a conference with the family, so that the family does not feel compelled to compare their child to others in the class.

Why Should You Document?

There are several important reasons for using documentation in early childhood classrooms.

Getting Started with Documentation

How do you document children's learning in ways that integrate with your teaching? Start by asking "What am I taking photos of? What am I noting about children's work and play?" Document instances that relate to your curriculum goals—what you plan to teach and how you promote the children's general development.

Here are examples of questions to consider while documenting:

> Do the child's physical skills, such as climbing, balancing, pouring milk, and holding a crayon, match those of other children his age?

> Does he make friends and play appropriately with other children?

> Has he begun to recognize letters or write them?

> Does he explore at the water table, learning about measuring, sinking, and floating?

Documenting these items for each child lets you know if he is meeting goals for physical and social and emotional development, literacy, and science learning. Use this information to plan your daily activities and monthly themes for the whole group. You can also use it to identify which children may benefit from more individual attention so they can work on particular skills. If a child's abilities seem far behind most children's his age, you and your director may want to discuss with the family whether the child could benefit from a thorough developmental assessment by an assessment professional.

Your group observations can spark ideas for rearranging your classroom or outdoor learning spaces to help the children learn better. Are there materials and equipment you could add that would better promote their development? How could you adjust your daily routines or teaching methods to engage more of the children in active learning?

Taking photos and notes, especially if you plan carefully and do it regularly, can be a powerful tool that pays off in improved family engagement, enhanced child learning, and your growth as a teacher!

(From Hedges 2016)

Showing Accountability

Accountability is one reason for documentation. Teachers are accountable to administrators, families, community members, and others, and documentation helps to provide evidence of children's learning. In addition, documentation can improve relationships, teaching, and learning. Use of this tool helps educators get to know and understand children, and it allows them to reflect on the effectiveness of their teaching practices (Alasuutari, Markström, & Vallberg-Roth 2014).

Extending the Learning

Consider the following example of how one thoughtful teacher could use documentation to prolong and extend an unexpected learning opportunity. A group of children finds some miscellaneous nuts and bolts on a playground, and their teacher, noting their curiosity, carefully observes their responses and listens to and documents their conversations (by using written notes, photographs, and video). She listens to learn what the children know about the items and what they wonder, such as "Where do these come from?" Then she facilitates a conversation with the children to learn more about their ideas and theories behind the purpose of the nuts and bolts and how they came to be on the playground.

Later the teacher incorporates the initial comments, the photographs, and the conversations in a documentation source (panel, website, PowerPoint, or other creative product). The children and teacher revisit the encounter through the documentation and reflect on the experience, which helps the children continue their conversation and drives forward their interest. This back-and-forth examination of the documentation helps the teacher and children negotiate a curriculum that is based on the children's interests (Seitz 2006).

Making Learning Visible

When expected to provide evidence that children are meeting learning standards, documentation is a natural way to make learning visible. Helm, Beneke, and Steinheimer (2007) call this idea *windows on learning*, meaning that documenting offers an insight into children's development and learning. Moreover, they observe, "Documentation can also assist the teacher in making decisions about when the additional support systems are needed for a child. As a teacher becomes a skilled documenter, he can improve his knowledge and skills" (12).

How Should You Document?

The documentation process is best done in collaboration with other teachers, parents, and in some cases, children soon after the experience. The information and product become richer when two or more teachers, children, and parents work together to understand an event. Collaboration also helps build a classroom community, which is important because it engages teachers, parents, and children in thinking about the process of learning.

When two or more people discuss an event, each brings a different perspective and a new level of depth. For example, teachers discussing a possible change to the classroom environment might bring up aspects that are necessary and that work as well as things they would like to change based on the children's needs, such as repositioning the furniture. Together they share how they have observed young children using the space. The resulting environment plan would look very different if just one individual had created it. Carlina Rinaldi discusses this notion of working together and building community: "To feel a sense of belonging, to be part of a larger endeavor, to share meanings—these are rights of everyone involved in the educational process, whether teachers, children, or parents...working in groups is essential" (1998, 114).

Stages in Learning to Document

First and foremost, documentation is a process that is learned, facilitated, and created in stages. Documenters actually go through their own stages as they learn more about documenting and using documentation to support their ideas. Many early childhood educators already document children's development and learning in many ways, and most communicate a variety of messages in diverse formats to families (Stacey 2015).

There are six stages that most early childhood educators, including college students and student teachers, move through both individually and collaboratively (see "Stages of the

Stages of the Documenter Experience

Stage	Experience	Value
1. Deciding to document	Documenters ask, "What should I document?" They collect artwork from every child but at first tend to create busy bulletin boards with too much information. Concerned with equity, many include every item rather than being selective.	Documenters show pride in the children's work.
2. Exploring technology use	Documenters explore various media platforms to display observations, photographs/videos, and artifacts, as different platforms highlight varying elements of the documentation. They keep in mind the importance of safety measures and photo information releases.	Documenters work hard to learn more about technology. They show pride in the children's actions by displaying photos and video clips.
3. Focusing on children's engagement	Documenters learn to photograph specific things and events with the intent of capturing a piece of the story of children engaged in learning.	Documenters become technologically competent and able to focus on important learning events and experiences.
4. Gathering information	Documenters title the photographs, events, and experiences and begin to write descriptions that tell the story of children's learning.	Documenters begin to connect children's actions and experiences.
5. Connecting and telling stories	Documenters combine work samples, photographs, descriptions, and miscellaneous information in support of the entire learning event. They involve children in selecting and discussing pieces the children feel are important to include. They tell the whole story with a beginning, middle, and an end, using supporting artifacts.	Documenters continue to use documentation artifacts to connect children's actions and experiences to curriculum and learning standards.
6. Documenting decision making	Documenters frame questions, reflect, assess, build theories, and meet learning standards, all with the support of documentation.	Documenters become reflective practitioners who document meaningful actions/events, explain why they are important, and push themselves and others to continue thinking about these experiences.

Culturally Responsive Teaching and Connections with Documentation

The power of documentation is that it tells a story in a way that shows in-depth learning, growth, and connections for children about the world around them. Each story can and should be meaningful to the documenter, the child, the family, and other audience members. These stories are windows into the workings of the classroom community and can be particularly effective at highlighting the strengths and diversity found within that community. A culturally responsive teaching approach values all children's cultures and experiences and uses them as a springboard for learning. A culturally responsive teacher learns about others' values, traditions, and ways of thinking and shares them with children, families, and other school members through documentation.

There are many benefits of documenting the cultural strengths within the classroom community. When children and families see themselves and others like them in the photographs, videos, and words on documentation panels or class websites, they know that others value their practices. It also helps children connect their families with others as they see similarities to others in the classroom. When a family's expertise is reflected in documentation, they feel like part of the experience and valued members of the classroom community. Social and emotional connections between children, families, and teachers are strengthened, and children and families are excited to be at school.

To promote a culturally responsive setting, document activities and learning that connect to

› Children's and families' backgrounds, heritages, and traditions, including foods and celebrations

› The learning environment (the place)

› School and family events

› Authentic curriculum

› Characteristics and talents of community members

› Children's home languages

Documenter Experience" on page 55). Educators who collaborate to learn more about documentation tend to have more positive experiences than those who work on their own.

Conclusion

Documentation can be a rewarding process when educators understand the value associated with collecting evidence and producing a summary presentation, whether in a bulletin board, panel, video, or other format. To become a documenter, one must first understand what to observe and what to do with the information collected. It takes time and practice to learn which experiences support effective documentation and how to collect artifacts and evidence.

Next, as documenters learn why the information is important, they begin to understand the value of documentation for different audiences and come to recognize why certain aspects of child development are important to assess. In addition, documenters learn that administrators and parents value this information, yet it also has value to the children and the teacher in planning authentic curriculum that meets children's needs.

Finally, the documenter learns how best to interpret and display the information gathered. Often the documentation provides insights into children's thinking and helps drive the future curriculum. Deepening children's learning is the ultimate reward of documentation.

References

Alasuutari, M., A.-M. Markström, & A.-C. Vallberg-Roth. 2014. *Assessment and Documentation in Early Childhood Education.* New York: Routledge.

Hedges, S. 2016. "Observing and Documenting." *Teaching Young Children* 9 (3): 32.

Helm, J.H., S. Beneke, & K. Steinheimer. 2007. *Windows on Learning: Documenting Young Children's Work.* 2nd ed. New York: Teachers College Press.

Reflection Questions

1. Think about the things that make each child you work with unique. How could you best document those characteristics? How could you share them with the child and her family?

2. What types of experiences in the classroom—such as group collaboration, literacy development, or science experiments—highlight children's strengths and their abilities to learn together? How might you use social media to share these experiences with families and administrators? What precautions do you need to take when using social media in this way?

3. How can you use your documentation of individual children and the classroom community to guide your curriculum planning?

Rinaldi, C. 1998. "Projected Curriculum Construction Through Documentation—Progettazione." In *The Hundred Languages of Children: The Reggio Emilia Approach—Advanced Reflections*, 2nd ed., eds. C. Edwards, L. Gandini, & G. Forman, 114. Greenwich, CT: Ablex.

Seitz, H. 2006. "The Plan: Building on Children's Interests." *Young Children* 61 (2): 36–41.

Stacey, S. 2015. *Pedagogical Documentation in Early Childhood: Sharing Children's Learning and Teachers' Thinking*. St. Paul, MN: Redleaf Press.

Resources

Curtis, D., & M. Carter. 2013. *The Art of Awareness: How Observation Can Transform Your Teaching*. 2nd ed. St. Paul, MN: Redleaf Press.

Curtis, D., D. Lebo, W.C.M. Cividanes, & M. Carter. 2013. *Reflecting in Communities of Practice: A Workbook for Early Childhood Educators*. St. Paul, MN: Redleaf Press.

Davies, B. 2014. *Listening to Children: Being and Becoming*. New York: Routledge.

Derman-Sparks, L., D. LeeKeenan, & J. Nimmo. 2015. *Leading Anti-Bias Early Childhood Programs: A Guide for Change*. New York: Teachers College Press; Washington, DC: NAEYC.

Forman, G., & B. Fyfe. 2012. "Negotiated Learning Through Design, Documentation, and Discourse." In *The Hundred Languages of Children: The Reggio Emilia Experience in Transformation*, 3rd ed., eds. C. Edwards, L. Gandini, & G. Forman, 247–71. Santa Barbara, CA: Praeger.

Hammond, Z. 2015. *Culturally Responsive Teaching and the Brain: Promoting Authentic Engagement and Rigor Among Culturally and Linguistically Diverse Students*. Thousand Oaks, CA: Corwin.

Lewin-Benham, A. 2015. *Eight Essential Techniques for Teaching with Intention: What Makes Reggio and Other Inspired Approaches Effective*. New York: Teachers College Press; St. Paul, MN: Redleaf Press.

Michael-Luna, S. 2013. "What Linguistically Diverse Parents Know and How It Can Help Early Childhood Educators: A Case Study of a Dual Language Preschool Community." *Early Childhood Education Journal* 41 (6): 447–55.

Wurm, J. 2014. *MORE Working in the Reggio Way*. St. Paul, MN: Redleaf Press.

About the Author

Hilary Seitz, PhD, is a professor of early childhood education at the University of Alaska Anchorage. Her research focuses on twenty-first century teaching pedagogies for teachers of young children, including culturally responsive teaching, integrated curriculum, authentic assessment, and connecting to the community.

Photographs: p. 50, © Vera Wiest; p. 54, © Getty Images

Facing the Challenge of Accurately Assessing Dual Language Learners' Learning and Achievement

Linda M. Espinosa

Accurately assessing young dual language learners' development and achievement is essential to providing appropriate, individualized instruction and improving the quality of education they receive (Espinosa 2008; Espinosa & Garcia 2012; National Academies of Sciences, Engineering, & Medicine 2017). Individualized instruction enhances young children's learning opportunities and promotes the important developmental and achievement outcomes necessary for school success.

Sections of this article are adapted from Espinosa 2014 and Espinosa & Gutiérrez-Clellen 2013.

Individualized instruction, however, requires comprehensive, ongoing assessments that are fair, valid, and linguistically, culturally, and developmentally appropriate (NRC 2008). Such assessments show educators how children are progressing and what educational decisions need to be made.

Many challenges exist for early childhood educators in accurately assessing dual language learners' learning and development. This article provides an overview of some of these challenges and the knowledge and skills that early childhood assessors—whether teachers or other professionals trained in assessing young children—need to meet them.

Understanding Features of Dual Language Learners' Development that Affect Accurate Assessment

Accurate assessment of dual language learners requires teachers to consider the unique aspects of linguistic and cognitive development that are associated with acquiring two languages during early childhood—as well as the larger social and cultural contexts that influence children's overall development (Espinosa & Gutiérrez-Clellen 2013). While all young children are capable of learning and benefiting from two languages (Bialystok & Feng 2011; Paradis, Genesee, & Crago 2011), important individual and contextual differences may affect dual language learners' development of knowledge and skills that are essential for school success.

For example, dual language learners in the United States are much more likely than monolingual children to have parents without a high school education, to be raised in families with low income, and to be raised in cultural contexts that may differ from middle-class norms (Capps et al. 2005; Castro et al. 2014; Crosnoe 2005; Espinosa 2007; Hernandez 2006). All of these factors affect school performance. In addition, dual language learners' school performance and progress in learning English may vary due to

> Differences in home language experiences (Hammer, Scarpino, & Davison 2011)

> Timing and reasons for family immigration (Portes & Rumbaut 2005)

> Age of first exposure to English (Hammer, Scarpino, & Davison 2011)

> Differences in cultural beliefs and child socialization practices across families (Castro et al. 2014; Laosa 2006)

School administrators and teachers must consider the impact of all of these factors on each child and how they influence assessment results, then carefully determine how to best promote language skills and academic learning. Most current assessments of kindergarten readiness and academic progress do not consider the unique developmental strengths and needs of dual language learners and therefore consistently underestimate their language

A common feature of dual language learners' development is *code switching* (switching languages for portions of a sentence) and *language mixing* (inserting single items from one language into another) (Paradis, Genesee, & Crago 2011). In some cases, children mix the two languages in one communication because they do not yet have sufficient vocabulary in one language to fully express themselves.

Code switching and language mixing are natural processes that have been linked to growing proficiency in both languages (Paradis, Genesee, & Crago 2011). Assessors therefore need to consider *all* of the child's knowledge, across both languages, when judging her abilities.

abilities and conceptual knowledge. Assessment should include information from families about their child and the home language environment.

Determining What a Dual Language Learner Knows

Undertaking the assessment of dual language learners involves looking at both their level of English language development and their learning in their home language (National Academies of Sciences, Engineering, & Medicine 2017).

Identifying the Language to Use for Assessment

Becoming proficient in a language is a complex, challenging process that takes many years for children of all ages (Hakuta, Bialystok, & Wiley 2003). As children acquire a second language, one language may be more dominant because they use that language more often than the other at a particular point in time. If dual language learners are assessed only in their least proficient language (usually English), their conceptual knowledge and true language abilities will be underestimated. Therefore, a teacher should assess a child both in his home language and in English—first in the language he uses most frequently and prefers.

When there are no valid assessment instruments available in the child's home language, early childhood assessors need to collaborate with the family and collect important information about the child's early language experiences and typical usage to determine whether the child is functioning at age-appropriate levels in the home language. The Office of Head Start publication *Gathering and Using Language Information that Families Share* provides detailed guidance on what information to collect, how to collect it, and why it is useful (National Center on Cultural and Linguistic Responsiveness 2017). See particularly the section "Collecting Information from the Families of Dual Language Learners."

Identifying a Child's Stage of English Language Development

If a child has limited English skills, this will likely affect her performance on any early childhood assessment. To accurately determine whether a dual language learner's language abilities are at age-appropriate levels, educators need a working knowledge of the stages of second language acquisition during the early years. Most children learning more than one language progress through several stages of fluency as they gradually learn more English (Espinosa & Gutiérrez-Clellen 2013). Understanding a child's level of English language development will help teachers interpret the child's language abilities and apply assessment results. For example, if a dual language learner is in the earliest stage of acquiring English and has had very little prior exposure to English, the teacher would not expect the child to speak in complete sentences when responding to an English prompt during testing or ask the child to talk in English during large group activities.

Assessing a Child's Knowledge in Each Language

Before teachers can determine a dual language learner's developmental status, educational progress, or need for educational intervention, it is necessary to understand what the child knows in each of her languages. She may know some words and concepts in one language and other words in the second language. Depending on her experiences and learning

opportunities, she may not perform as well as monolingual speakers of each language in all domains. This is a typical and, most often, temporary phase of emergent bilingualism (Paradis, Genesee, & Crago 2011). A child who demonstrates difficulties in both languages, however, should be referred for further evaluation to determine whether she needs additional services.

Working with the child's family, early childhood assessors should develop a language profile of the child's strengths and needs that includes both background information and assessment data about the child's language skills in both languages.

Understanding the Specific Purpose for Assessment

The purpose of an assessment must guide assessment decisions. For example, assessment strategies used by teachers for daily instructional purposes are typically less formal than assessment strategies employed by administrators for program accountability or evaluation purposes. While there are several broad purposes for assessing young children (NRC 2008), early childhood practitioners need to thoroughly understand how to accurately assess for the purposes of (1) promoting individual children's learning and development and (2) identifying and referring children who may have delays or disabilities. Each of these purposes requires particular assessment instruments, procedures, and technical standards and carries a potential for cultural and linguistic bias. It is critical that assessors understand the unique considerations and recommendations for—and particularly the limitations of—assessing dual language learners for each purpose (see "Limitations of Standardized Assessments with Dual Language Learners" on page 64).

Observational Assessment for Promoting Learning

Carefully observing dual language learners' interactions and language use can provide important information about their level of language development. This type of assessment is often referred to as *authentic,* meaning that ongoing observations of children's behavior and use of language over time in the natural classroom environment are less contrived than standardized testing and, if aligned with curriculum goals, can be critical to instructional planning. Frequent assessment for instructional improvement and adjustment includes observations during everyday activities, checklists, rating scales, work samples, and portfolios (Espinosa 2008). Observations and insights from other staff members who speak the child's home language and have contact with the child—for example, family engagement specialists or health specialists—can be collected through standardized questionnaires or family interviews (Espinosa 2006).

Early childhood assessors should observe and carefully document dual language learners' behavior and language across the day in different activities, including outdoors and during interactions with peers, and look for which language the child uses when and with whom. These observations should be organized around curriculum goals, focus on the most important outcomes, include information from multiple sources gathered over time, and include families (NAEYC 2005; NAEYC & NAECS/SDE 2003).

For children who are in the early stages of English acquisition, it is crucial that someone who is proficient in the children's home language determine their understanding of mathematical concepts, their social skills, and their progress in the other developmental domains. Unless an assessor is fluent in the child's home language and properly trained to conduct the assessment, it is not possible to obtain accurate results. For example, a teacher who does not understand the language a child is using when speaking to a peer would find it difficult to determine if that child is displaying empathy for others on the playground.

Assessment for Identifying Children with Potential Delays or Disabilities

Developmental screening is the process of identifying young children who may be at risk of cognitive, motor, language, or social and emotional delays and who require further assessment, diagnosis, and/or intervention. A large number of young Latino children and other dual language learners with delays or disabilities are not identified (NCES-IES 2007). In later grades, children who speak a language other than English at home and are not fully

proficient in English often are *overrepresented* in special education, particular those in low-income communities (Rueda & Windmueller 2006). Clearly, there is a need to improve the methods used for screening dual language learners who may require special services.

Typically, brief standardized developmental screenings are administered to large numbers of children to determine if there is a potential problem and whether referral for more in-depth assessment is warranted. Standardized instruments allow for comparisons of one child's development against that of similar children and are often used to determine if the child is developing within normative ranges. However, most standardized screening tools have not been designed or normed with young bilingual children and have serious limitations.

Other factors impact the testing situation and results with dual language learners. Most teachers and assessment professionals have not been trained to conduct unbiased assessments with children from culturally and linguistically diverse backgrounds, and many do not speak the child's home language and are unfamiliar with the home culture. Many teachers lack knowledge of the psychometric characteristics of tests and therefore cannot make informed judgments about the appropriateness of specific tests for children from linguistically diverse backgrounds. Also, it can be difficult for educators to distinguish between *language differences* attributable to growing up with two languages and *language delays*, which may require specialized language interventions (Espinosa & Lopez 2007).

For all of these reasons, it is important for those who assess dual language learners to employ multiple measures and sources of information, consult with a multidisciplinary team that includes bilingual experts (e.g., speech therapists and psychologists who speak the child's home language), collect information over time, and include family members in the screening process (Barrueco et al. 2012; Espinosa & Lopez 2007). A child who demonstrates difficulties in both languages should be referred for an evaluation to determine the need for additional services.

Steps to Follow in Assessing Young Dual Language Learners

Specific questions can guide the assessment process to ensure accurate results are obtained (Espinosa & Gutiérrez-Clellen 2013):

1. **Does the child speak a language (or languages) other than English at home?** This can be determined through a family interview or questionnaire. If the child uses or is exposed to only English at home, all assessments can be conducted in English. If the child speaks another language, informal and formal assessments must be conducted in both languages.

2. **What is the child's level of English language development?** For most dual language learners, the early childhood curriculum will need to focus on oral language development, early literacy skills, and writing targeted to the individual child's level of English language development. If the child is in an early stage of learning English, her language skills are likely to affect her academic readiness if they are not sufficiently supported.

3. **What are the child's development and skills in her home language?** If the child exhibits limited home language development, this may indicate a risk of developmental language delay, and a referral for an evaluation should be made. If the child shows age-appropriate competencies in her home language, teachers should support her continued development in that language to help her maintain those skills and prevent loss of the home language.

4. **What is the teacher's opinion of the child's learning progress and potential?** By observing the child during learning activities across different times of the day, teachers can evaluate the child's engagement and comprehension during these interactions. Comparing the child's responsiveness to that of other dual language learners can also provide critical information about a child's learning progress and potential. Children who have limited English skills but are highly responsive to peer and adult interactions are likely to be successful learners given opportunities for multiple language-learning interactions.

Limitations of Standardized Assessments with Dual Language Learners

When using any assessment measure with dual language learners, proceed with caution. Here's why:

› Most assessments were designed and normed on populations of children who speak only English, so they may not be appropriate for children who speak more than one language.

› Most early childhood assessments that have been translated from English into another language have not been re-normed, and they report validity and reliability data only from the English versions of the assessments.

› Many translated assessments are not equivalent to the English versions in terms of language difficulty, nor do they capture cultural meanings.

› Few trained bilingual assessors are available to administer standardized measures in both English and another language.

› Assessment results often underestimate dual language learners' total vocabulary knowledge.

Therefore, when early childhood assessors are required to administer standardized tests to dual language learners, it is vital that they understand the psychometrics of the instruments and collaborate with fully bilingual professionals who have knowledge of the child's culture. Then, they need to interpret the results *cautiously*. The results may not be an accurate reflection of children's language skills or conceptual knowledge, as the tests may not be valid for children who speak a home language other than English.

5. **Are there any developmental concerns affecting the child's learning that need to be addressed directly?** To answer this question, it is critical to select assessment measures that are culturally and linguistically appropriate. Only screening instruments that are administered in the two languages (if both are spoken) will reveal whether a true delay or disability exists. If appropriate instruments are used and the child shows delays in both languages, a full evaluation will be necessary to develop an individualized intervention.

6. **What knowledge and skills does the child have in each language?** Conducting assessments in both the child's home language and English will yield a fuller picture of what he knows and can do. This information is critical to planning instructional activities.

Conclusion: What Teachers and Program Staff Need to Know to Conduct Valid Assessments

Educators assess dual language learners' development and achievement in order to individualize instruction, improve the quality of education, and improve academic school readiness. This multistep process requires knowledge of certain aspects of the linguistic and cultural development of dual language learners as well as the specific characteristics of the assessment instruments administered. Educators need to understand the stages of English language development and the importance of continuing to build on children's home languages for their overall language development and future academic achievement. They also need to be skilled in authentic assessment methods related to curriculum goals and linking ongoing assessment results to individualized instruction.

The ability to make judgments about the developmental, cultural, and linguistic appropriateness of available instruments will enable educators to make the best decisions about the use of specific assessments for dual language learners (see Barrueco et al. 2012 for a discussion of strengths of early childhood assessments available in Spanish and English). Administrators must provide the necessary support for teachers to acquire these competencies and make these judgments.

When reviewing assessment results, educators need to understand the limitations of standardized instruments used with dual language learners and use their professional judgment when interpreting and applying the assessment results. Assessment in early childhood education is a process that requires teams of individuals who all contribute specialized information about the child; therefore, it is important that staff be skilled in team collaboration. Finally, all staff members must be competent in working across cultures to establish effective reciprocal relationships with diverse families. Armed with this knowledge and support, early childhood practitioners must "continue to use their best judgment, wisdom, and practical knowledge to make decisions about how to effectively assess and use assessment results for each child" (NAEYC 2005, 12) and can successfully face the challenge of accurate assessment of dual language learners.

References

Barrueco, S., M. López, C. Ong, & P. Lozano. 2012. *Assessing Spanish-English Bilingual Preschoolers: A Guide to Best Approaches and Measures*. Baltimore: Brookes Publishing.

Bialystok, E., & X. Feng. 2011. "Language Proficiency and Its Implications for Monolingual and Bilingual Children." In *Language and Literacy in Bilingual Settings*, eds. A.Y. Durgunoglu & C. Goldenberg, 121–38. New York: Guilford.

Capps, R., M. Fix, J. Murray, J. Ost, J.S. Passel, & S. Herwantoro. 2005. *The New Demography of America's Schools: Immigration and the No Child Left Behind Act*. Research report. Washington, DC: The Urban Institute. www.urban.org/sites/default/files/publication/51701/311230-The-New-Demography-of -America-s-Schools.PDF.

Castro, D., E. Garcia, L. Espinosa, F. Genesse, C. Gillanders, C. Hammer, D. LaForett, E. Peisner-Feinberg, & P. Tabors. 2014. "Conceptual Framework for the Study of Dual Language Learners' Development." Unpublished manuscript, Microsoft Word file.

Crosnoe, R. 2005. "Double Disadvantage or Signs of Resilience? The Elementary School Contexts of Children from Mexican Immigrant Families." *American Educational Research Journal* 42 (2): 269–303.

Espinosa, L.M. 2006. "Social, Cultural, and Linguistic Features of School Readiness in Young Latino Children." In *School Readiness and Social-Emotional Development: Perspectives on Cultural Diversity*, eds. B. Bowman & E.K. Moore, 33–47. Washington, DC: National Black Child Development Institute.

Espinosa, L.M. 2007. "English Language Learners as They Enter School." In *School Readiness and the Transition to Kindergarten in the Era of Accountability*, eds. R.C. Pianta, M.J. Cox, & K.L. Snow, 175–96. Baltimore: Brookes Publishing.

Espinosa, L.M. 2008. *Challenging Common Myths About Young English Language Learners*. Advancing PK–3, No. 8. Policy brief. New York: Foundation for Child Development. www.fcd-us.org/assets/2016/04 /MythsOfTeachingELLsEspinosa.pdf.

Espinosa, L.M. 2014. "Perspectives on Assessment of DLLs' Development & Learning, Prek-Third Grade." Commissioned paper presented at the National Research Summit on the Early Care and Education of Dual Language Learners, in Washington, DC.

Espinosa, L.M., & E. García. 2012. *Developmental Assessment of Young Dual Language Learners with a Focus on Kindergarten Entry Assessment: Implications for State Policies*. Working Paper #1. Center for Early Care and Education Research–Dual Language Learners (CECER-DLL). Chapel Hill, NC: The University of North Carolina, Frank Porter Graham Child Development Institute. http://cecerdll.fpg.unc .edu/sites/cecerdll.fpg.unc.edu/files/imce/documents/CECER-DLL_WP%231_Nov12.pdf.

Espinosa, L.M., & V.F. Gutiérrez-Clellen. 2013. "Assessment of Young Dual Language Learners in Preschool." In *California's Best Practices for Dual Language Learners: Research Overview Papers,* eds. F. Ong & J. McLean, 172–208. Sacramento, CA: Governor's State Advisory Council on Early Learning and Care.

Espinosa, L.M., & M.L. López. 2007. "Assessment Considerations for Young English Language Learners Across Different Levels of Accountability." Los Angeles: The National Early Childhood Accountability Task Force; Los Angeles: First 5 LA. www.pewtrusts.org/~/media/legacy/uploadedfiles/wwwpewtrustsorg/reports /pre-k_education/assessment20for20young20ellspew2081107finalpdf.pdf.

Hakuta, K., E. Bialystok, & E. Wiley. 2003. "Critical Evidence: A Test of the Critical-Period Hypothesis for Second-Language Acquisition." *Psychological Science* 14 (1): 31–8.

Hammer, C.S., S. Scarpino, & M.D. Davison. 2011. "Beginning with Language: Spanish-English Bilingual Preschoolers' Early Literacy Development." In Vol. 3 of *Handbook of Early Literacy Research,* eds. S.B. Neuman & D. Dickinson, 118–35. New York: Guilford.

Hernandez, D.J. 2006. *Young Hispanic Children in the U.S.: A Demographic Portrait Based on Census 2000.* Report to the National Task Force on Early Childhood Education for Hispanics. Tempe: Arizona State University.

Laosa, L.M. 2006. *Preschool Program Effects on Hispanic Children's Cognitive Development: Is Pre-K Preparing Hispanic Children to Succeed in School?* New Brunswick, NJ: National Institute for Early Education Research.

NAEYC. 2005. "Screening and Assessment of Young English-Language Learners." Supplement to the NAEYC and NAECS/SDE Joint Position Statement on Early Childhood Curriculum, Assessment, and Program Evaluation. Washington, DC: NAEYC. www.naeyc.org/sites/default/files/globally-shared/downloads /PDFs/resources/position-statements/ELL_Supplement_Shorter_Version.pdf.

NAEYC & NAECS/SDE (National Association of Early Childhood Specialists in State Departments of Education). 2003. "Early Childhood Curriculum, Assessment, and Program Evaluation: Building an Effective, Accountable System in Programs for Children Birth Through Age 8." Position statement. Washington, DC: NAEYC. www.naeyc.org/sites/default/files/globally-shared/downloads/PDFs/resources /position-statements/CAPEexpand.pdf.

National Academies of Sciences, Engineering, and Medicine. 2017. "Promising and Effective Practices in Assessment of Dual Language Learners' and English Learners' Educational Progress." In *Promoting the Educational Success of Children and Youth Learning English: Promising Futures,* eds. R. Takanishi & S. Le Menestrel, 402–30. Washington, DC: National Academies Press. doi:10.17226/24677.

National Center on Cultural and Linguistic Responsiveness. 2017. *Gathering and Using Language Information that Families Share.* Grant document prepared for the US Department of Health and Human Services, Administration for Children and Families, Office of Head Start (Project No. 90HC0001). Washington, DC: Office of Head Start. https://eclkc.ohs.acf.hhs.gov/sites/default/files/pdf/gathering -using-language-info-families-share.pdf.

NCES-IES (National Center for Education Statistics, Institute of Education Sciences). 2007. *The Condition of Education 2007.* Washington, DC: US Department of Education. https://nces.ed.gov/pubs2007/2007064 .pdf.

NRC (National Research Council). 2008. *Early Childhood Assessment: Why, What, and How.* Washington, DC: National Academies Press. doi:10.17226/12446.

Paradis, J., F. Genesee, & M.B. Crago. 2011. *Dual Language Development and Disorders: A Handbook on Bilingualism and Second Language Learning.* 2nd ed. Baltimore: Brookes Publishing.

Portes, A., & R.G. Rumbaut. 2005. "The Second Generation and the Children of Immigrants Longitudinal Study." *Ethnic and Racial Studies* 28 (6): 983–99.

Rueda, R., & M.P. Windmueller. 2006. "English Language Learners, LD, and Overrepresentation: A Multiple-Level Analysis." *Journal of Learning Disabilities* 39 (2): 99–107.

About the Author

Linda M. Espinosa, PhD, is professor emerita of early childhood education at the University of Missouri, Columbia and has served as the codirector of the National Institute for Early Education Research (NIEER) at Rutgers University and vice president at Bright Horizons Family Solutions. Her recent research and policy work have focused on effective curriculum and assessment practices for young children from families with low income who are dual language learners.

Photographs: pp. 58, 61, 62, © Getty Images; p. 63, © Bob Ebbesen

Portfolio Picks

An Approach for Developing Children's Metacognition

Elida Velez Laski

As a kindergarten teacher, I felt there was never enough time in the school day to accomplish everything I wanted to. There was so much for the children and me to explore, to learn, and to share that it was hard having to stop and assess their learning with the standardized assessments that my district expected me to administer. Portfolio assessment was different, however. The portfolios told the story of all that we had done over the year, they were a source of pride for me and the children, and perhaps most important, these assessments seemed to extend the children's learning rather than interrupt it. Years later, as a professor of education who teaches courses in cognition and learning, I have a better understanding of why portfolio assessment felt right to me as a teacher. Portfolio assessment not only documents learning but also can help children in preschool, kindergarten, and the primary grades develop a critical tool for learning—their own metacognition.

Benefits of Portfolio Assessment

Portfolios are systematic collections of children's work, artifacts, and teachers' notes that capture children's learning over time. Portfolio assessment offers an authentic approach to assessment that is developmentally appropriate (Harris 2009; Seitz & Bartholomew 2008). Like other forms of assessment, portfolio assessment gives teachers information about how to adjust their teaching and about the kinds of experiences that might be most helpful to individual children. Unlike standardized assessments, portfolio assessment allows multiple opportunities and ways for children to demonstrate their understanding of concepts and ideas. Another advantage of portfolio assessment over standardized assessments is that it can communicate progress and learning in ways that are easier for families to understand (Gelfer 1994). Portfolios provide evidence of progress that is more apparent and often more meaningful to parents than a percentile score on a test. For example, portfolios can easily show improvements in children's writing skills from October to May.

From my experience, the most important benefit of portfolio assessment is that it provides children an opportunity for self-assessment. If children are included in the selection of their portfolio pieces, they can review their work, talk about their thinking process that occurred during the work, discuss their interests and habits, and make choices about which pieces to include. Portfolios also offer children a way of understanding their own progress. In my classroom, children often looked through their portfolios during choice time and commented on their own progress. One child looking through his writing samples said with a giggle, "Look! Remember when I didn't know how to spell *mom?* Now I can write *dinosaur!*" The opportunities portfolio assessment provides for children to engage in self-assessment are exactly the kinds of experiences that have been found to support the early development of metacognition—an aspect of cognition recognized as critical for learning (Larkin 2010).

What Is Metacognition?

Metacognition refers to "thinking about thinking," such as knowing what we know or do not know, monitoring the outcomes of our work, setting goals, and planning ahead (Dunlosky & Metcalfe 2009). Children and adults with better metacognition tend to have higher academic achievement and be more successful (Larkin 2010). Better metacognition is also associated with greater reading comprehension; more coherent, elaborate writing; and better mathematics problem solving. Essentially, children with good metacognitive skills are self-directed learners who are able to self-evaluate and select new strategies when appropriate rather than rely on someone else to guide them (Bransford, Brown, & Cocking 2000). Thus, children with better metacognition get the most out of learning opportunities. For example, they monitor their comprehension as they read, notice when they do not understand something, and then do something about it, such as reread or seek help (Baker 2016). These behaviors allow them to learn more when they independently read books.

Like most other cognitive skills, metacognition develops slowly throughout childhood and into adolescence (Schneider 2008). Yet even 3-year-old children are capable of some forms of metacognitive thought (Lyons & Ghetti 2010). Children as young as 2½ years can comment on when they know or do not know something, such as when asked the name of an object. Between the ages of 3 and 5 years there is substantial improvement in children's ability to accurately reflect on the certainty of their memories, using words such as *know*, *think*, and *forget*. This improvement is one indicator of an increasing awareness of knowledge states and the ability to reflect on the accuracy of their thinking. In time, children can monitor and regulate their thinking *during* a task and plan appropriately *before* a task. Children over the age of 5, for example, switch strategies more often than preschoolers during a task when their current strategy is not working.

While metacognition improves with age, it also can be developed through explicit training (Dignath, Buettner, & Langfeldt 2008). Teachers and families can promote children's metacognition by asking them to articulate their thinking during a task. For example, while doing a puzzle with a kindergarten child, simply asking "How did you figure out where that piece belongs?" can help him learn to monitor and reflect on his own thinking. Teachers and families can also promote children's metacognition by asking them what they know about a topic, how they learned it, and what they want to know about it.

Portfolio Picks

Selecting pieces for portfolios offers the perfect opportunity to probe children's thinking about their work. Initially, it might seem overwhelming to involve children in the selection of their portfolio pieces, but I found that with just a little planning and organization it was quite manageable. In fact, studies have found that children as young as preschool age can be involved productively in the development of their portfolio (Gelfer & Perkins 1996; Seitz & Bartholomew 2008).

One way to involve children is to make the process a regular part of the classroom routine, culture, and environment. To do this, my coteacher and I developed Portfolio Picks. This became the name of a yearlong bulletin board in the classroom that celebrated children's work and their reflections about that work, and also the name of monthly conferences dedicated to selecting the pieces that would be displayed.

Once a month, I met with small groups of three or four children, sometimes over the course of a day and other times over the course of a week. During the conferences, children looked through their "finished work" folder where they kept work or artifacts (such as a sign a child created for a block structure) completed each day. I talked with each child in turn, discussing his work and selecting one piece that would be displayed on the bulletin board. As children's new pieces were posted, the previous ones were transferred to their portfolio folders. In addition to the pieces selected with the children, I added other items to their portfolios to ensure that they contained multiple kinds of evidence—my anecdotal notes, results of formal assessments, and other artifacts that I selected independently.

Using Portfolio Assessment to Promote Children's Metacognition

My strategies for helping children select appropriate portfolio pieces and to assess their own work changed over the course of the year as children exhibited greater ability to critically evaluate their work. Initially, I took most of the responsibility in guiding the child to a particular piece and describing why I thought it was a good choice. Gradually, I transferred that responsibility to the child. My role changed from leading the child's thinking to eliciting and facilitating her thinking to finally observing and commenting on her thinking.

Thus, over the course of the year, I used three general strategies for supporting children's selection of portfolio pieces and promoting children's metacognition:

1. Model and Think Aloud

2. Conference and Coconstruct

3. Independent Self-Assessment and Articulation of Thinking About Thinking

Each of these strategies differs in terms of its purpose and benefits to the child (Dignath, Buettner, & Langfeldt 2008). (See "Strategies for Supporting Children's Selection of Portfolio Pieces and Promoting Metacognition" on page 72.) The purpose of the first strategy, Model and Think Aloud, is primarily for the teacher to model her own thinking. This approach provides children with an example of how to reflect on their work and also helps them acquire specific language that they can use to talk about their thoughts and evaluate their work, such as *hard, confusing, proud,* and *notice* (Bransford, Brown, & Cocking 2000; Larkin 2010). The purpose of the second strategy, Conference and Coconstruct, is to provide children with reflection questions they can ask themselves. These questions promote metacognitive discourse, which helps children become aware of their own thinking. The purpose of the third strategy, Independent Self-Assessment and Articulation of Thinking About Thinking, is to provide children with an opportunity to take on the responsibility for assessing their own work, to articulate and explain their self-assessment, and to set their own learning goals. This approach helps children see themselves as responsible for their own learning and feel validated for their metacognitive efforts.

While I typically used these strategies sequentially, the rate at which I moved through them was not the same for every child. Some children continued to need more scaffolding than others, such as some dual language learners who needed more modeling and thinking aloud until they developed the language to be able to comment on their own work. Sometimes I used more than one strategy during a child's conference. For instance, I might begin a conference by having the child do an independent self-assessment. However, if I notice that the child seems to focus only on apparent or relatively superficial features of the work, such as the neatness of the handwriting, I might shift to the Model and Think Aloud strategy and comment on the complexity of the sentence structure in order to help the child to continue to develop more sophisticated forms of self-assessment.

These general strategies are consistent with approaches that have been found to promote metacognition. For example, there is much evidence that one way to support children's metacognition is by modeling the kind of thinking you want to promote (Dignath, Buettner, & Langfeldt 2008; Larkin 2010). Teachers can let children "see" their thinking processes by thinking aloud and describing their own reasons for selecting portfolio pieces.

The following examples from a kindergarten classroom demonstrate the three strategies for promoting children's self-assessment.

Model and Think Aloud: Pamela's Menu

Pamela's conference occurred near the beginning of the year. She seemed timid and had a limited oral vocabulary. Thus, the teacher guided her toward a menu that Pamela had created with the teacher the day before and used the opportunity to model the self-assessment process.

Strategies for Supporting Children's Selection of Portfolio Pieces and Promoting Metacognition	
Model and Think Aloud	The teacher takes the lead and models her thinking process by making comments on the child's work. For example, ■ "Hmmm. I notice that on this work you included many details and chose your colors carefully. This seems to be a great example of being very thoughtful in your work." ■ "I know that you have been working really hard on sounding out words. I wonder if there's a piece in here that shows that. Oh, look at this work!" ■ "This math work is interesting. What I notice is that you did a lot of erasing. That tells me that you noticed when an answer didn't seem right. I think this would be a great example because it shows how you are learning to fix your own mistakes."
Conference and Coconstruct	The teacher elicits the child's thinking about his work and recasts or elaborates on his ideas through prompts and leading questions. For example, ■ "Tell me about this piece you selected. Why are you proud of it?" ■ "Do you remember doing this work? What parts do you remember thinking really hard about?" ■ "Do you notice something you did on this work that you couldn't do before? I notice that . . ." ■ "You said you like the letters you wrote. Do you mean you like how carefully you wrote the letters or that you remembered to use some lowercase letters?" ■ "You said, 'It's beautiful.' Tell me more. What do you think makes it beautiful? How did you come up with that idea?"
Independent Self-Assessment and Articulation of Thinking About Thinking	The child takes the lead, and the teacher builds on her "thinking about thinking" with comments. For example, ■ "Tell me more about what you learned from doing this work." ■ "So, what do you think you can do better? What might be a goal?" ■ "You are really thinking about what you had to think about when you were doing the work, not just what it looks like!" ■ "Based on what you noticed, how would you approach a work like this differently next time?"

Teacher: I think this piece would be a good choice for your portfolio.

Pamela: Yeah—I like it.

Teacher: I think it is a good choice because it is a really nice example of your writing. You needed a menu, and you decided to make one yourself! That was really good problem solving.

Pamela: (*Giggles and nods.*)

Teacher: I also remember that when you were figuring out how to write the words, like *menu*, you were saying them very slowly to try and hear all the sounds.

Pamela: (*Nods and smiles.*)

Teacher: I also noticed that you made a lowercase *b* and *e*. We've talked about trying to use lowercase letters more, and you did it here!

Pamela: (*Nods and smiles again.*)

Teacher: Hmm . . . so what do you think we should write about this work? (*Pauses between each question.*) Why are you proud of it? What does it show you have learned?

Pamela: I made a little *e*.

Teacher: OK. I'll write, "I'm proud of this work because I wrote a lowercase *e*."

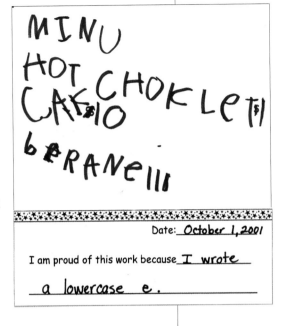

In this example, the teacher takes the lead in selecting a piece and describing why it is a good choice. She also carefully models the kind of language that is central to metacognition and self-assessment, such as *remember*, *noticed*, and *proud*. This type of interaction helps children understand the various aspects that are important to consider, such as achieving the goal of writing lowercase letters and developing the vocabulary to communicate their own thoughts and ideas about their work.

Conference and Coconstruct: Alessandra's Picture of Stars and Moons

Alessandra's conference took place near the middle of the year. As she looked through the pieces in her finished work folder, she gravitated toward a writing sample in which she had drawn several moons and stars and had written, "The moon and stars make the world shine." Noticing her interest in this piece, the teacher decided to focus the conference on it.

Teacher: So, tell me. Why did you choose this work? Why are you proud of it?

Alessandra: Because I made it.

Teacher: What do you mean by that?

Alessandra: Because I drawed it and I drawed the words.

Teacher: Can you tell me something about the words that you are proud of?

Alessandra: Sounding out.

Teacher: Do you remember which word was hard for you?

Alessandra: I listened carefully [to the sounds] in *moon*.

Teacher: I noticed you also remembered how to spell your expert word *the*.

Alessandra: Yeah, and I writed all the letters by myself.

Teacher: OK, we'll add this piece to your portfolio. It shows a lot of thinking and how much you are growing as a writer!

Culturally and Linguistically Appropriate Assessment

Portfolio assessment is a method of assessment that honors the differences across children. The process of selecting portfolio pieces described in this article enables children to focus on their strengths and express what is important to them; it also encourages them to learn to identify areas for future practice and development. In supporting this process, teachers can choose a strategy for helping children select their work that is sensitive to linguistic differences. Children may need more or less guidance in assessing their own work, particularly when it comes to using language to do so in their speech and in their writing. Dual language learners, for example, may especially benefit from the teacher modeling her thinking process aloud, emphasizing the language necessary for engagement in metacognition. It may also be helpful when the teacher highlights words such as *know, think,* and *forget* by repeating them frequently when introducing the Portfolio Picks activity to the class and using them in individual conferences with each child.

Teachers can consider encouraging children to express themselves in either their home language or English (or both) when reflecting on their work. Children who are able to choose the language(s) they use to describe their thinking about their own work will likely feel more comfortable speaking about it. This will ultimately help them develop the skills necessary to think about their own thoughts, knowledge, and goals and eventually to share these metacognitive reflections with others. In addition, Portfolio Picks that make use of children's home languages can be beneficial because children may find it easier to share their work and their self-assessments with their family members in their home language.

Regardless of the language children use in their Portfolio Picks, this form of assessment helps them recognize their accomplishments and set new learning goals. In this way, portfolio assessment benefits children from diverse backgrounds in ways that standardized assessment cannot.

Supporting Children with Delays or Disabilities

Portfolios are a great tool for demonstrating progress for children with delays or disabilities because there are so many options for individualization. The portfolio can be entirely strengths-based and focused on the child's individualized goals and learning. Because this approach to assessment reflects a child's individual growth rather than what he is or isn't doing compared to peers, it is meaningful to both teachers and families.

Using portfolio assessment to promote metacognition in children with disabilities may require significant scaffolding. You might need to spend more time using the Model and Think Aloud strategy and focus on just one or two specific attributes of the work. Select a work for the child, or offer two examples for the child to choose from. For a child with an intellectual disability, you might use a simple prompt about each piece ("Which drawing makes you feel proud?") and

note his response, even if it's a nod or a gesture. For a child with limited vocabulary or expressive language, provide visual cues like pictures of facial expressions to help her communicate how she feels about a piece of work. Consider having the child reflect on her work shortly after completing it while the experience is still fresh and meaningful.

Above all, as you gather work for the portfolio, make sure it accurately reflects what the child can do. Children with disabilities are not always able to demonstrate their skills in ways that are easily captured on paper. Be creative! Use photos of the child engaged in activities like constructing puzzles or participating in circle time, or consider creating a digital portfolio with video clips and photos of work products. Having the child respond to these images of himself will keep the reflection process more concrete and the reaction more authentic.

In this example, the teacher encourages the child to evaluate her own work. She follows the child's lead about which piece to discuss and begins by asking the child to describe why it is a good choice for her portfolio. Throughout the interaction, however, the teacher plays a key role in helping elicit and expand the child's thinking and comments. This kind of interaction helps children develop more sophisticated forms of self-assessment and metacognitive language through scaffolding as more responsibility is passed to them.

Independent Self-Assessment and Articulation of Thinking About Thinking: Josephine's Research from the Science Center

Josephine's conference occurred toward the end of the year. Prior to meeting with the teacher to discuss her work, she had independently selected a butterfly piece. She completed it after observing live butterflies in the science center and using books in the center to identify the parts of a butterfly.

Teacher: So, tell me. Why did you choose this piece?

Josephine: Well, I'm proud of it because I wrote all the parts of the butterfly.

Teacher: OK. What else?

Josephine: Well, I learned some parts of the butterfly I didn't already know.

Teacher: Great. So this work shows what you have learned in science. When you look at this piece, do you see something that you still need to work on? Or something that you might try to do better next time?

Josephine: Hmm. I could write a little neater, like keep on the lines. The e and the s are off the lines.

Teacher: Your handwriting has come a long way, but I think that is a good goal to keep working on.

In this example, the child takes the lead in evaluating her work. She independently selects the piece she wants to discuss and identifies its strengths and potential areas for improvement. The teacher's role is to allow the child the opportunity to articulate her self-assessment and to validate her thoughts. This kind of interaction helps children view themselves as responsible for monitoring their own learning and setting their own goals.

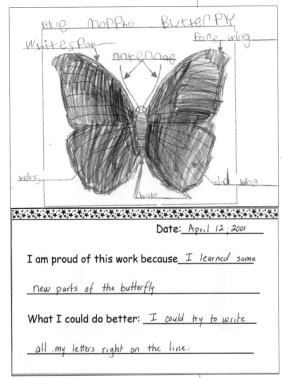

Date: April 12, 2001

I am proud of this work because I learned some new parts of the butterfly

What I could do better: I could try to write all my letters right on the line.

Reflection Questions

1. The article discusses some of the benefits of portfolio assessment. What other benefits can you think of?

2. How can you guide children in recognizing good options for their portfolios?

3. How will this guidance change over the course of the school year or vary from child to child?

4. The article discusses three strategies for supporting children's selections and promoting metacognition. How will you determine when a child is ready to progress to the next strategy?

5. Think about the planning and organization you need to do to ensure a Portfolio Picks activity goes smoothly in your classroom. What can you start implementing?

Conclusion

As early childhood educators, we want to develop children's skills and content knowledge, but we also want to help them take the initiative for their own learning. Involving children in the selection of their portfolio pieces offers them opportunities to develop their metacognitive skills. Through portfolio assessment we can both document children's learning in our classrooms and help prepare them to be self-directed learners in the future.

References

Baker, L. 2016. "The Development of Metacognitive Knowledge and Control of Comprehension: Contributors and Consequences." In *Improving Reading Comprehension Through Metacognitive Reading Strategies Instruction,* ed. K. Mokhtari, 1–32. Lanham, MD: Rowman & Littlefield.

Bransford, J.D., A.L. Brown, & R.R. Cocking, eds. 2000. *How People Learn: Brain, Mind, Experience, and School.* Expanded ed. Washington, DC: National Academies Press. www.nap.edu/catalog.php?record_id=9853.

Dignath, C., G. Buettner, & H. Langfeldt. 2008. "How Can Primary School Students Learn Self-Regulated Learning Strategies Most Effectively? A Meta-Analysis on Self-Regulation Training Programmes." *Educational Research Review* 3 (2): 101–29.

Dunlosky, J., & J. Metcalfe. 2009. *Metacognition.* Thousand Oaks, CA: SAGE Press.

Gelfer, J.I. 1994. "Implementing Student Portfolios in an Early Childhood Program." *Early Child Development and Care* 97 (1): 145–54.

Gelfer, J.I., & P.G. Perkins. 1996. "A Model for Portfolio Assessment in Early Childhood Education Programs." *Early Childhood Education Journal* 24 (1): 5–10.

Harris, M.E. 2009. "Implementing Portfolio Assessment." *Young Children* 64 (3): 82–5.

Larkin, S. 2010. *Metacognition in Young Children.* New York: Routledge.

Lyons, K.E., & S. Ghetti. 2010. "Metacognitive Development in Early Childhood: New Questions About Old Assumptions." In *Trends and Prospects in Metacognition Research*, eds. A. Efklides & P. Misailidi, 259–78. New York: Springer.

Schneider, W. 2008. "The Development of Metacognitive Knowledge in Children and Adolescents: Major Trends and Implications for Education." *Mind, Brain, and Education* 2 (3): 114–21.

Seitz, H., & C. Bartholomew. 2008. "Powerful Portfolios for Young Children." *Early Childhood Education Journal* 36 (1): 63–8.

About the Author

Elida Velez Laski, PhD, is an associate professor at Boston College's Lynch School of Education. Elida worked as a teacher and district coach for more than eight years. She conducts research on the application of cognitive science to teaching practice and teaches courses related to child development and learning.

Effective Kindergarten Readiness Assessments

Influencing Policy, Informing Instruction, and Creating Joyful Classrooms

Elliot Regenstein, Maia C. Connors, Rio Romero-Jurado, and Joyce Weiner

In far too many kindergarten classrooms, teachers feel intense pressure to develop instructional activities that will drive up children's scores on mandated assessments—including, ironically, readiness assessments. With good intentions, but often inadequate knowledge of child development, some leaders have enacted kindergarten assessment and accountability policies that are neither appropriate nor productive. But, as the authors of this article explain, others have done just the opposite. Working with educators, some leaders have found that kindergarten readiness assessments—used regularly, but without high stakes—can support joyful, playful learning and inform state-level decision making (such as which communities should receive additional resources).

As the other articles in this book demonstrate, teachers who cultivate joyful learning honor both the fundamentals of early childhood and the need to further children's growth and development. That means building on children's interests, providing time for exploration, and engaging with children's stories and dramatic play (and more!). It also means deeply understanding the content areas, closely observing children's current knowledge and abilities, and carefully planning appropriately challenging learning environments and activities.

To be responsive to children's needs, teachers must frequently and systematically collect information on children's growing knowledge, skills, and interests across academic, social, and emotional domains. It's a daunting task. But as this article shows, policymakers and administrators can help by providing well-informed, flexible guidelines on kindergarten readiness assessments. Used as snapshots of current abilities (not as tools for accountability), these assessments help teachers design lessons, centers, and projects that are engaging, meaningful, and joyful for every child.

As assessment becomes more common in early childhood, teachers, administrators, and policymakers should work together. This article on sensible, supportive, flexible uses of kindergarten readiness assessments can provide a model and will hopefully spur needed discussions.

—Lisa Hansel, Editor in Chief, Young Children

I n the Valley View Community Unit School District, four kindergarten teachers—Stephanie Eick, Patsy Guzman, Shannon Lunardini, and Ashley Volland—have been on the cutting edge of implementing Illinois' kindergarten readiness assessment for the past several years. If you ask them about the impact of the assessment on their classroom practice, they will all give the same answer: it has led to more joy, more play, and more student learning.

Across the country, state policymakers and district leaders are increasingly seeking to implement kindergarten readiness assessments because they provide valuable information about the skills that children bring with them when they enter school. Used wisely, they help teachers, schools, districts, and states understand how to better support children's development. Ideally, every school district would experience these new assessments as useful tools that inform instruction. The key lesson learned in Valley View's implementation is important: teachers need time and support to get adjusted to kindergarten readiness assessment practice—and if they have that time and support, they can use the assessment results to create rich, engaging learning environments that are well matched to children's needs and interests.

As early childhood education policy analysts and researchers, we have analyzed the use of kindergarten readiness assessment results throughout the United States and the potential impacts of using those results for improper purposes. Our paper, "Uses and Misuses of Kindergarten Readiness Assessment Results" (Regenstein et al. 2017), offers a detailed

Improving Practice

Excerpted from "Uses and Misuses of Kindergarten Readiness Assessment Results"

As early learning systems have grown and matured, there has been an increase in the use of kindergarten readiness assessments (KRAs) that measure where children are developmentally as they transition into kindergarten. Kindergarten readiness assessments have been a valuable tool for leaders and practitioners to identify gaps in children's knowledge and skills and to enhance teaching and learning.

Within the broad category of improving practice, there are numerous specific efforts that KRAs can support:

> KRA results can be used to develop "ready schools"—that is, schools that are well-designed to meet the needs of their incoming kindergartners. Using KRAs in a school can inform a community conversation about the needs of the incoming kindergarten cohort, which can inform early learning program design and transition planning for children and families.

> KRAs can support early learning and kindergarten classrooms in aligning their practices by informing teachers about the overall strengths and weaknesses of each cohort's skills at kindergarten entry, in order to better target instruction and strengthen transitions.

> KRAs can also support teachers' understanding of children's learning and advance their knowledge of child development as they document each child's knowledge and competencies and identify a child's strengths and areas in need of improvement.

> KRAs can also foster teacher–parent partnerships. Families can be included as part of the process of sharing what they know about their child's learning and also receive information about their child's development that can support learning needs at home.

> KRAs can provide useful information—along with results from screenings and other observations—to identify children who should be referred for evaluation of potential developmental delays or other special needs.

Successfully implementing KRAs for any instructional purpose requires ongoing training and supports for teachers conducting the assessment; teachers administering the assessment should not only be trained on the tool(s) being used but also knowledgeable in child development, children's capabilities and cultural and linguistic backgrounds, and guiding principles for assessment. Teachers also need training in how to use assessment data in order to make decisions and plan activities to support child improvement. Conducting ongoing cycles of assessment to inform instruction is time consuming for teachers and resource intensive for schools, and it demands that school leaders protect the time necessary to do the work correctly if the results are to be meaningful. Thus, an intentional investment and recognition of the benefits by administrators and teachers are imperative for meaningful formative use of KRAs to improve instruction.

Ensuring Equity in Kindergarten Readiness Assessments

Developing and implementing a kindergarten readiness assessment that accurately assesses young children coming from culturally, linguistically, and ethnically diverse backgrounds is critical considering the value of KRAs in guiding practice, identifying an individual child's abilities and needs, and informing policies and resource decision making. Given the limited number of assessment instruments that have been designed or adapted with these populations in mind, experts have noted important considerations and challenges to ensuring validity and reliability in assessments. For example, young dual language learners may be assessed in multiple languages, which raises issues around assessment availability in other languages and the cultural familiarity and language skills of the assessor. Assessors need to be fluent in both English and the preferred or dominant language of the child and have appropriate versions of the same assessment to be able to administer the assessment effectively. Moreover, assessors need training on the indicators of typical language development for children speaking another language and guidance on how best to report and interpret such results from multiple languages, and they must be knowledgeable about the children's cultural and community contexts. These considerations, along with others experts have identified, must continue to be explored and addressed to ensure valid findings and well-guided policy decisions that are equitable and truly benefit young children.

This excerpt offers a small sample of the full paper, which is available for free online. For a more detailed look at the benefits of kindergarten readiness assessments, an important discussion of why these assessments should not be used to make high-stakes decisions, and extensive references, go to www .theounce.org/wp-content/uploads/2017/03 /PolicyConversationKRA2017-1.pdf.

analysis of why some uses of kindergarten readiness assessment results are appropriate and others are not (see "Improving Practice" on page 79). Here, we discuss the most essential issues surrounding classroom- and school-level uses of these assessments, drawing on both our paper and our informative interviews with the kindergarten teachers in Valley View.

What Is Kindergarten Readiness?

For educators to assess kindergarten readiness, it has to be defined. Fortunately, in most states there is a formalized operating definition of kindergarten readiness (Connors-Tadros 2013; Regenstein et al. 2017). While those definitions vary, there are a few characteristics that are common across states:

> Readiness encompasses multiple domains of growth and development. State early learning standards generally take this into account by addressing a wide range of domains (Early Childhood Education Research Alliance 2013; Education Commission of the States 2014; Regenstein et al. 2017). The exact names of domains may vary, but they generally include concepts like language and literacy, cognition, general knowledge (including early science and mathematics concepts), approaches to learning, physical well-being and motor development, and social and emotional development (Regenstein et al. 2017; Shepard, Kagan, & Wertz 1998).

> Young learners develop skills and abilities across all of these developmental domains in a highly interrelated manner, building confidence and expertise as new competencies are mastered. But children often progress unevenly within and across domains, meaning that ongoing observations may be needed to get a sense of a child's developmental trajectory (Regenstein et al. 2017; Snow 2011).

> Similarly, there is high variability in what is considered the "normal range" of child development (Meisels 2006; NAEYC 2009). Young children are constantly developing and acquiring new skills, but the rate at which early learners acquire new concepts and skills varies significantly among children.

Although some states do not have a formal definition of kindergarten readiness, they all have a de facto definition of kindergarten readiness in their learning standards. That is, all 50 states have learning standards that cover the prekindergarten years and are articulated to some degree by standards for kindergarten (Education Commission of the States 2014; Regenstein et al. 2017). These learning standards from both early learning and K–12 provide a guide to educators about what kindergarten readiness should look like.

Once kindergarten readiness has been defined, it can be measured. And in the Valley View district—where the assessment is implemented well and the results are used to enhance the learning environment—that is where the fun begins. Neither teachers nor children feel pressure; in fact, teachers find that the assessment helps them identify children's interests and develop activities that help children grow.

Assessing Kindergarten Readiness

"Students don't realize they're being assessed in any way," says Ms. Volland. Assessment tools will generally ask teachers to evaluate children in multiple domains. An initial assessment will occur in the fall as children begin their kindergarten year, and the best tools call for additional evaluations throughout the school year. Gathering information

only at the beginning of the school year may not give teachers a complete understanding of each child's abilities. To ensure an accurate picture of children's growth over time, multiple opportunities should be provided for teachers to gather child data throughout the academic year and for children to demonstrate the developmental, social and emotional, and cognitive progress that they are making (CCSSO 2011).

While each of the four Valley View kindergarten teachers uses some different approaches, a few common themes have emerged. These include

> Assessing children during center time, rather than one on one, because it feels more natural to the children.

> Inquiring about the children's activities. The teachers approach children who are already working on something and start asking questions about it. As Ms. Guzman says, they are "learning while they are playing." She adds that she will ask them questions about what they are doing that build on their areas of interest.

> Using technology, such as a tablet, to record answers and take photos of what they are seeing in their classroom. One teacher also uses an app to organize the evidence by domain.

> Soliciting feedback from physical education teachers, librarians, music and art teachers, and specialists who work with individual children, such as speech therapists, to get a richer sense of how the children are developing.

At Valley View, the teachers expressed enthusiasm for the assessment tool they use—the Kindergarten Individual Development Survey (KIDS) (ISBE 2018). The teachers discussed ways that KIDS helped them understand the strengths and needs of the children they teach, which in turn allowed them to develop activities that added joy to the classroom. It also strengthened collaboration among teachers—when a strategy for ramping up the fun was a hit in one classroom, it quickly spread to others.

Across the country, there is a wide range of assessment tools in use, and consensus is still emerging on the state of the art in kindergarten readiness assessment. The National Research Council has recommended some best practices for assessment tools—including that they should be used by teachers in the classroom environment throughout the kindergarten year and to collect information on multiple domains of development (NRC 2008). In particular, it is important that assessments support equity—they must be designed to account for culturally, linguistically, and ethnically diverse backgrounds (Regenstein et al. 2017).

Even though there are many different kindergarten readiness assessment tools, there are two basic categories of uses for the results of those assessments: (1) improving practice at the school level and (2) analyzing system-wide needs at the policy level. Both are briefly discussed in the following sections.

Using Kindergarten Readiness Assessment Results to Improve Practice

"Data help us differentiate and give specific kids the help they need to progress," Ms. Lunardini says, adding that data also provide useful information to specialists at the school. Some of the specific benefits the teachers identified include

> Improving their ability to form successful groups within the classroom.

> Helping to identify interventions that might be beneficial to specific children, such as targeted instruction or a speech therapist.

> Gaining a better understanding of the social and emotional needs of the children. As Ms. Volland says, the assessment has helped her "get to know each student on a deeper level." Ms. Guzman adds that it has "broadened my way of looking at students."

> Understanding children's interests and preferences, including which children need more time to think before contributing to a discussion and which ones benefit from more hands-on activities.

Because the assessment required teachers to consider their students' problem-solving skills and ability to work together, the teachers universally reported that they were doing more to support those skills and abilities in the classroom—and that it was paying off. They reported that children were taking more initiative to solve problems among themselves, and were

How Assessments Contribute to Joyful Learning

While most educators probably do not equate kindergarten readiness assessments with increasing the joy in learning, they can be excellent tools for just that. These tips will help teachers and administrators maximize the benefits of their assessments:

> Use kindergarten readiness assessments to get to know the children better—not just their needs as learners, but also their emerging and long-term interests.

> Implement the assessments as a natural part of teachers' interactions with children; this will prevent children from feeling pressure and give teachers a more accurate picture of current strengths, needs, and opportunities.

> Engage a wide range of colleagues in the assessment process in order to more deeply understand each child. Also engage those colleagues in creating new, interdisciplinary learning opportunities for each child.

> Use frequent assessments as an opportunity to engage in new creative activities or try out innovative learning centers; the assessment results will help gauge the effectiveness of the new approaches and support reflection and refinement over time.

> Avoid misusing assessment results; while kindergarten readiness assessments inform instruction, they should not be used for high-stakes accountability (for children, teachers, or schools).

Becoming an Informed Advocate for Appropriate Assessment

Add your voice to those of other advocates committed to ensuring that assessment is beneficial for children and does not put them at risk from potentially harmful practices. Below are some recommendations.

Learn About Appropriate Assessment

Review research findings about the benefits of assessments based on careful observations of what children know and are able to do, as well as the potential harm that can come from inappropriate approaches to assessing young children. Here are a few resources:

› *Early Childhood Assessment: Why, What, and How*, National Research Council (National Academies Press, 2008). doi:10.17226/12446

› "Early Childhood Curriculum, Assessment, and Program Evaluation" (NAEYC position statement developed in collaboration with NAECS/SDE). NAEYC.org/sites/default/files/globally-shared /downloads/PDFs/resources/position-statements /pscape.pdf

› *Developing Kindergarten Readiness and Other Large-Scale Assessment Systems: Necessary Considerations in the Assessment of Young Children,* Kyle Snow (NAEYC, 2011). https://issuu.com/naeyc/docs /assessment_systems

› Materials from advocacy groups such as the National Black Child Development Institute (www.nbcdi.org) and Defending the Early Years (www.deyproject.org) can help you stay up to date on current developments and get involved in public efforts relating to appropriate assessments.

Engage in Advocacy in Your School and Community

› Engage in collegial dialogue about effective assessment practices with fellow teachers and school administrators.

› Articulate your position clearly to let the school community know what you believe and why. Help other teachers, families, and community members understand that multiple measures provide a better sense of a child's development and help to shape effective curriculum.

› Join together with others to speak out about appropriate assessment strategies and uses of assessment results.

› Help policymakers understand the benefits of assessment when done well and the potential risks to young children when assessments or their results are used inappropriately.

› Write to your local media about the need for appropriate testing practices.

› Present workshops or panels about assessment issues at a local AEYC affiliate meeting or a meeting of another association concerned with early childhood education.

› Provide written or oral testimony regarding legislation on assessing young children.

(From Feeney & Freeman 2018)

---

learning more independently. One teacher even reported that sometimes when a student was asking her a question, another student would jump in to help answer.

A more challenging area for the teachers was communicating results to families. The teachers acknowledged the tricky balance of giving families more specific, child-centered information than they were receiving before without overwhelming them with too much data. While the teachers have had the benefit of training in how to analyze the data, families have not. The teachers thought the reports produced from their assessment were potentially too dense for families to understand easily, and teachers' individual efforts to work around that challenge have not been consistently successful. Moreover, the teachers found that some families were expecting feedback from teachers to be focused on what the families think of as "academic" development, but the teachers thought it was important to discuss with families their newfound perspective on the children's growing social and emotional skills. To improve communication with families, Illinois recently developed a website (www.isbe.net/kids) with more information on the assessment.

System-Wide Measurement of Kindergarten Readiness

States are increasingly looking to use kindergarten readiness assessments as a system-wide measurement of children's strengths and needs when they enter kindergarten. Maryland has been a pioneer in this area, using data from kindergarten readiness assessments to help inform early learning investments (Regenstein et al. 2017). Because it is so difficult for schools to help students catch up when they fall behind grade-level expectations, schools, districts, and states should use these assessment results to proactively address the common challenges found within groups of incoming kindergartners (Regenstein et al. 2017).

As valuable as this information can be, it is important that the results of kindergarten readiness assessments not be misused. Some potential *misuses* of the information include the following:

> Using individual kindergarten readiness scores to hold a child back or prevent a child from enrolling in kindergarten

> Holding individual early learning programs accountable for the results their former students produce on kindergarten readiness assessments

> Measuring the quality of teaching, or holding teachers accountable for the kindergarten readiness of their students

No existing kindergarten readiness assessments were designed for any of these purposes—and for the latter two in particular, there are a host of measurement challenges that make using the assessment results unreliable and inappropriate for those purposes (Regenstein et al. 2017). There are important differences between kindergarten readiness assessments and the accountability assessments that begin in third grade, so just because they are all called "assessments" does not mean that they can all be used in the same ways. Simply put, the kindergarten readiness assessments currently available cannot be used for accountability purposes.

Supporting Effective Implementation

"Everyone has to participate in the training process," Ms. Eick says. For administrators and teachers in Valley View, maximizing the benefits of their assessment is an ongoing effort that has already been in effect several years. The Valley View teachers have learned some important lessons that can make the assessment process more joyful and effective in other districts as well:

> **Take it one step at a time.** Ms. Lunardini noted that her team worked on literacy the first year, then math the next. That approach provided time to master the different elements of the assessment.

> **Do not expect to get everything right the first time.** Ms. Volland noted that she had tried various ways of keeping data; it took her many iterations to come up with a system she really felt comfortable with. She has shared her tools with other teachers to help them speed up the process, but she knows that all teachers have to figure out what works for them.

> **Work together.** Ms. Guzman emphasized that partnership and mentorship among teachers are essential.

While teachers can do a lot to help each other, they also need leadership and support from administrators. Many principals have limited experience with the development of

young children; according to a survey by the National Association of Elementary School Principals, most principals who are early in their careers feel like they could improve their understanding of child development (Education Week 2015; Loewenberg 2015). Indeed, if principals come to the job primarily with experience teaching older children, they might not know what great kindergarten instruction really looks like (Szekely 2013). In particular, they may not appreciate the importance of creating a joyful learning environment, including building on children's interests through centers, guided play, and free play.

The Valley View teachers noted that implementing KIDS helps their administrators really understand what it means for teachers to do great work with young children. One principal provided supplies like play kitchens and tool sets to support play in the classroom; another even said "a noisy classroom is a learning classroom" because children should be talking with each other. Ms. Eick explained that principals were increasingly understanding that play can include purposeful play-based learning in curricular activities aligned with the standards, and that it is a false dichotomy to talk about learning and play as two separate things (Hassinger-Das, Hirsh-Pasek, & Golinkoff 2017).

Beyond training on child development, successfully implementing kindergarten readiness assessments for any instructional purpose requires ongoing training and support for teachers conducting the assessment. To be effective, teachers need to be trained on how to administer the tool and on how to then use the data to support children's learning and development (Guss et al. 2015). Conducting ongoing cycles of assessment to inform instruction requires a meaningful investment of time and resources. The payoff can be worth it, but for the results to be useful, school leaders and teachers must protect the time necessary to do this work carefully and completely.

Culturally and Linguistically Appropriate Assessment

Kindergarten readiness assessments can be a useful tool to help teachers meet the needs of a culturally and linguistically diverse student population. For that to happen, however, those assessments need to be appropriate for the population being assessed. Not all kindergarten readiness tools are validated for dual language learners, so states, districts, schools, and teachers all need to be sure that any assessments they use are appropriate for the populations being assessed and are administered in a culturally and linguistically responsive manner.

If teachers are using a valid assessment, a number of critical practices will help ensure meaningful results with dual language learners:

› Conduct assessments in both the child's home language and English. Assessments that allow children to use all of their linguistic resources will yield the most reliable data. If you don't speak the child's home language, partner with another adult who does and who is trained in administering kindergarten readiness assessments. This individual does not need be a teacher, and schools with diverse populations might consider how best to train support personnel to administer and interpret assessments.

› Solicit information about a child from his family, and conduct observations across multiple settings. Gathering information from a variety of sources leads to more complete assessment results. Observations should take place in settings that are natural for the child and sensitive to his cultural background; this will elicit more authentic language—the way the child typically speaks in an informal setting—and give you a more accurate measurement of the child's capabilities.

› Realize that dual language learners follow a different developmental trajectory than monolingual English speakers (Espinosa 2017). Some children's total vocabulary may be larger than that of their peers, but it is divided across two languages. For many, their receptive English skills are stronger than their expressive English skills. Recognize that strong skills in the child's home language are critical to developing corresponding skills in English.

› Be cautious in interpreting the results of a single assessment. High variability is normal in kindergarten readiness assessment, including for dual language learners. The complexities of assessing dual language learners can make it challenging for teachers to avoid under- or over-identifying children for developmental delays. It may be wisest to treat the initial results as a hypothesis that is continually monitored and observed, particularly when you are assessing children from a cultural background with which you are unfamiliar.

Kindergarten readiness assessments present a valuable opportunity for teachers to learn about the children in their classrooms, so it is important that states, districts, and school leaders provide the necessary supports for teachers to implement them effectively. When implemented well, these assessments can yield valuable information that supports improved instruction for dual language learners and all children.

All of the Valley View teachers acknowledged that it had taken them several years to master the assessment process. The Valley View teachers agreed that the perspective of teachers who have been through the process before can be helpful to those just starting out. In schools that are trying these kinds of assessments for the first time, bringing in some of those experienced voices could be very helpful. In schools where assessments are already up and running, experienced teachers should be given time to mentor the newer teachers.

Conclusion

For Valley View's teachers, kindergarten readiness has changed how they do business. It is "not a shift away from rigorous instruction, but a different way of providing it," as Ms. Eick puts it. These four teachers and their colleagues are leveraging assessment to create a more joyful classroom by learning how to better observe their students, collecting information about how their students are learning, and then using that information to inform instruction. Because kindergartners love to learn, good kindergarten readiness assessments will help teachers understand children's strengths and challenges as well as keep up with their natural curiosity and respond to their social and emotional needs.

Moreover, the experiences of teachers and principals with kindergarten readiness assessment should help inform policy choices that increase support for the education of young children, in kindergarten and earlier. Kindergarten classrooms benefit not only from teachers who understand how to help their students but also from children who come into them ready for what's ahead. Stronger investments in preschool and infant-toddler programs can give more children the educational opportunities they need.

Kindergarten readiness assessments can be a valuable resource for creating joyful classrooms where children's needs are met and interests are pursued. For these four Valley View teachers, the journey has been well worth it. With the right tools and supports, it can be worth it for many more teachers in schools around the country.

References

Connors-Tadros, L. 2013. "Overview of State Kindergarten Readiness Definitions." Center on Enhancing Early Learning Outcomes (CEELO) presentation to the Arkansas Kindergarten Readiness Indicators Committee, in Little Rock, Arkansas. http://ceelo.org/wp-content/uploads/2013/08/CEELO-AR-SchoolReadiness.pdf.

CCSSO (Council of Chief State School Officers). 2011. "Moving Forward with Kindergarten Readiness Assessment Efforts: A Position Paper of the Early Childhood Education State Collaborative on Assessment and Student Standards." Washington, DC: CCSSO. https://files.eric.ed.gov/fulltext/ED543310.pdf.

Early Childhood Education Research Alliance. 2013. "Implementing Early Learning Standards: Lessons from Research and Practice." Bridge webinar presented by Regional Educational Laboratory Northeast and Islands (REL-NEI) and Center on Enhancing Early Learning Outcomes (CEELO), April 14. www.ctearlychildhood.org /uploads/6/3/3/7/6337139/ecea-4-24-13-bridge-webinar.pdf.

Education Commission of the States. 2014. "50-State Comparison: Kindergarten Standards—General Info." http://ecs.force.com/mbdata/mbquestRT?rep=Kq1410.

Education Week. 2015. "New Principals: A Data Snapshot." *Education Week* 35 (1): 6. www.edweek.org/ew /section/multimedia/new-principals-a-data-snapshot.html.

Reflection Questions

1. How well do you understand your state's definition of kindergarten readiness? Is it well understood by your principal and teaching colleagues?

2. Once you collect information about students through the kindergarten readiness assessment, how do you leverage it to improve your instruction? How might your principal and teaching colleagues support you in this work?

3. How well do your school administrators understand effective instructional practices with children in kindergarten, first, and second grade? How can you use the assessment process to support their growing knowledge?

4. How effectively do you communicate with families about their children's kindergarten readiness assessment results and plans to support their children's continued learning? How might you do this more effectively?

5. Is the kindergarten readiness assessment used at your school implemented in ways that contribute to joyful learning? If not, what are the logical next steps to expand or improve implementation? If it is, what ongoing training and supports are available to you?

Espinosa, L.M. 2017. "KIDS Assessment and Dual Language Learners: Strengthening Data Collection and Application." Slide presentation at the Mastering KIDS Summit, Chicago, IL, December 14. www.isbe.net /Documents/DrLindaEspinosa.pdf.

Feeney, S., & N.K. Freeman. 2018. *Ethics and the Early Childhood Educator: Using the NAEYC Code*. 3rd ed. Washington, DC: NAEYC.

Guss, S.S., M. Sweet-Darter, B. Mangus, & A. Stein. 2015. *Measuring Data Utilization: A Report Examining Data Utilization Applicable to Educare Schools*. Literature review. www.ou.edu/content/dam/Education/documents /ECEI/Educare%20Data%20Utilization%20Literature%20Review%20revised%206-3.pdf.

Hassinger-Das, B., K. Hirsh-Pasek, & R.M. Golinkoff. 2017. "The Case of Brain Science and Guided Play: The Developing Story." *Young Children* 72 (2): 45–49. www.naeyc.org/resources/pubs/yc/may2017/case-brain -science-guided-play.

ISBE (Illinois State Board of Education). 2018. "KIDS: Every Illinois Child Ready for Kindergarten." Early Childhood Division. Accessed March 9. www.isbe.net/kids.

Loewenberg, A. 2015. "Many New Principals Lack Early Ed Knowledge." Education Policy. New America. www .newamerica.org/education-policy/edcentral/elem-principals-prek.

Meisels, S.J. 2006. "Accountability in Early Childhood: No Easy Answers." Occasional Paper 6. Herr Research Center for Children and Social Policy, Erikson Institute. www.erikson.edu/research/accountability-in-early -childhood-no-easy-answers.

NAEYC. 2009. "Developmentally Appropriate Practice in Early Childhood Programs Serving Children from Birth Through Age 8." Position Statement. Washington, DC: NAEYC. www.naeyc.org/sites/default/files/globally -shared/downloads/PDFs/resources/position-statements/PSDAP.pdf.

NRC (National Research Council). 2008. *Early Childhood Assessment: Why, What, and How*. Washington, DC: National Academies Press. doi:10.17226/12446.

Regenstein, E., M. Connors, R. Romero-Jurado, & J. Weiner. 2017. "Uses and Misuses of Kindergarten Readiness Assessment Results." Ounce of Prevention Fund. *Policy Conversations* 6 (1). www.theounce.org/wp-content /uploads/2017/03/PolicyConversationKRA2017-1.pdf.

Shepard, L., S.L. Kagan, & E. Wertz, eds. 1998. *Principles and Recommendations for Early Childhood Assessments*. Washington, DC: National Education Goals Panel. http://govinfo.library.unt.edu/negp/reports /prinrec.pdf.

Snow, K. 2011. *Developing Kindergarten Readiness and Other Large-Scale Assessment Systems: Necessary Considerations in the Assessment of Young Children*. Washington, DC: NAEYC. https://issuu.com/naeyc/docs /assessment_systems.

Szekely, A. 2013. "Leading for Early Success: Building School Principals' Capacity to Lead High-Quality Early Education." Washington, DC: National Governors Association. www.nga.org/files/live/sites/NGA/files /pdf/2013/1306LeadingForEarlySuccessPaper.pdf.

About the Authors

Elliot Regenstein, is a partner at Foresight Law + Policy. He was formerly the senior vice president for advocacy and policy at the Ounce of Prevention Fund.

Maia C. Connors, PhD, is a senior research associate for research and policy initiatives at the Ounce of Prevention Fund. Her research focuses on understanding early childhood care and education policies that support both adults' and young children's learning.

Rio Romero-Jurado, MA, is a policy specialist for the Ounce of Prevention Fund's national policy team. She supports the team's consultation to states as well as the collective policy and advocacy work of the Educare Learning Network.

Joyce Weiner is a policy manager with both the Illinois and national policy teams at the Ounce of Prevention Fund. She focuses on policy work that supports diverse, well-prepared teachers and administrators for the birth to 8 workforce.

Photographs: pp. 77, 81, 85, © Getty Images

Developing a Performance-Based Report Card

Teresa Wright and Barbara Murray

As a veteran kindergarten teacher with more than 25 years of experience, it is Mr. Byrne's practice to meet with each family to discuss their child's first report card. In recent years, this conference has become more meaningful because the school system adopted a new performance-based kindergarten report card that reflects both academic and develomental indicators of progress. Using the new progress report, Mr. Byrne can holistically evaluate each child based on standards and effectively exchange information with families.

The authors of *Ready or Not: Leadership Choices in Early Care and Education* write that before 2000, the "dominant context" for early childhood education was "children follow a natural developmental trajectory that is enhanced by a nurturing and supportive learning environment" (Goffin & Washington 2007, 60). High-quality early childhood programs focus on supporting young children's development of social, emotional, cognitive, and physical skills. The important concept that "all children in America will start school ready to learn," the first of eight goals in the Goals 2000: Educate America Act, created a shift in views on early learning, from an emphasis on "early care" to an emphasis on "early education" (NASDSE 1994, 3). According to Goffin and Washington (2007), scientific, social, educational, and economic factors supporting early education converged around the start of the twenty-first century, resulting in a renewed focus on the importance of high-quality early experiences as a predictor of future success, and on the realization that young children are capable of learning much more than previously thought possible. In response, many early childhood programs now focus on school readiness, closing the achievement gap, and preparing children for success in a global economy (Goffin & Washington 2007).

This shift led many US school districts to begin considering literacy and math to be priorities over all other content areas addressed in the early childhood years (Wilson 2009). The substantial accountability measures required by the No Child Left Behind (NCLB) Act of 2001 led to early childhood educators spending more time preparing children for testing on cognitive skills than addressing social, emotional, and physical development (Miller & Almon 2009).

In this article we share how the kindergarten program in the Brevard County, Florida, school district transitioned to a new performance-based report card. The new card supports teachers' use of developmentally appropriate practices rather than simply serving as a checklist for children's mastery of discrete, often isolated skills like the number of upper- and lowercase letters a child can name. The report card serves as official documentation of a child's progress in school. (Note that the terms *report card* and *progress report* are used interchangeably. They both refer to teachers' periodic reporting on children's progress, using a standardized school district form.)

Discontent with a Report Card

During frequent visits to kindergarten classrooms, the authors observe instruction and talk with teachers about their challenges in meeting the needs of children and their families. It was during such visits in 2008 and 2009 that teacher discontent with the school district's kindergarten report card came to light. This dissatisfaction was a result of frequent changes to Florida state standards and the limitations of the progress report as an effective tool for communication with families about their child's readiness for first grade.

Teachers expressed frustration with the report card's format, which showed children's progress according to certain academic skills but did not provide developmental indicators. Indicators such as adapting to new situations, exhibiting physical coordination and endurance, and comprehending information through listening would provide a more complete picture of a kindergartner's progress. The teachers explained that the format did not allow them to share the child's progress related to current Florida state learning standards for kindergarten. The report card emphasized assessing literacy and math skills without giving sufficient attention to social, emotional, and physical development, which are not addressed in state standards but are critical in determining a child's readiness for first grade. Further,

because the progress report focused on discrete skills, it was out of date in relation to the more global state learning standards adopted in 2007 and revised in 2012.

Teachers also expressed concern about the excessive amount of time needed to assess and record the numerous discrete skills listed in the report. The progress report required teachers to sit with each child individually to assess numerous isolated skills rather than approach the assessment from the more holistic perspective of looking at the skills and accomplishments of the whole child. The new report card format allows teachers to assess students through authentic means, such as direct observation and student work. Assessments can be done during individual, small group, and whole group instructional periods.

Transforming a Report Card

During the 2009–2010 school year, a report card committee—including school district resource teachers, school principals, kindergarten teachers, and the authors—worked together to develop a new performance-based report card. The disconnect between the report card in use at the time and the state education standards was so significant, it was clear that developing a new progress report for kindergarten was essential. To collect background information, the committee researched report card formats used by other school districts in Florida and surveyed administrators, teachers, and families. The committee then used these data in developing the school district's new progress report, to be implemented in the following school year, 2010–2011.

The committee's challenge was to develop a report card that effectively communicated children's progress in meeting the academic standards prescribed by the state while giving families insight into their children's progress in social, emotional, and physical development. The committee aimed to create a more inclusive progress report that could track children's abilities in both academic and developmental indicators. They also needed a report card that could be adapted, as necessary, to reflect changes in the state academic standards for kindergarten. The goal was to develop a reporting instrument that would give a family essential information about how their child was developing and progressing in relation to the expectations for kindergartners as expressed in the state standards and in terms of early childhood development.

Fostering Developmentally Appropriate Practices

School district staff learned that kindergarten teachers' expectations, defined by the original progress report, often worked in conjunction with state learning standards to determine what they taught. If certain learning expectations were listed on the report card, teachers addressed them as part of their daily instruction. For example, the previous report card placed a heavy emphasis on letter identification, so teachers devoted a great deal of time to helping children develop this isolated skill.

In addition, the fact that content areas were included on the report card added credibility to their importance as part of the kindergarten program. The original report card gave little credence to social, emotional, and physical development—the team knew they needed to restore these elements to the progress report. Primarily because the original report card emphasized literacy and math skills, the amount of classroom time allotted for activities that foster social, emotional, and physical development was reduced.

How did our team create a meaningful progress report that accurately reflects individual children's progress in the domains important in early childhood? The first step was to look to the NAEYC position statement on developmentally appropriate practice in early childhood programs. The statement outlines 12 principles of child development and learning (equally important, regardless of their numerical sequence) that inform practice for early childhood programs (NAEYC 2009).

Although all 12 principles are essential factors in providing developmentally appropriate programs for young children, the team leaned heavily on the following NAEYC principles to guide their decision making:

1. All the domains of development and learning—physical, social and emotional, and cognitive—are important, and they are closely interrelated. Children's development and learning in one domain influence and are influenced by what takes place in other domains.

2. Many aspects of children's learning and development follow well-documented sequences, with later abilities, skills, and knowledge building on those already acquired.

3. Development and learning proceed at varying rates from child to child, as well as at uneven rates across different areas of a child's individual functioning.

4. Development proceeds toward greater complexity, self-regulation, and symbolic or representational capacities. (11–12)

These four principles of child development, grounded in current early childhood research, provided the theoretical framework for the committee's decisions about the new report card content and the performance codes that would be used to indicate a child's level of mastery for each standard. Following the principles allowed the team to determine which domains to include and to present the desired standards as a hierarchy of skill development toward greater complexity as a child matures. In addition, it became clear that the performance codes used to communicate progress should reflect student growth and allow for the variance in the development of each child when compared not only to peers but across different domains. For example, one child may regularly exhibit complete mastery of a standard, while another may be progressing in achieving the standard but requires additional support from the teacher. Specific codes for identifying the variance in these abilities were needed.

Considering Performance Codes

The report card committee found determining the performance codes for the new report card to be particularly challenging. Committee members knew they did not want to use the previous indicators: *S* (successfully meeting the standards), *T* (time/support needed to consistently meet standards), and *N* (needs attention, not meeting standards). They also determined that the first and second grade report card indicators of *outstanding, satisfactory, needs improvement,* and *unsatisfactory* did not align with the theoretical framework because they are highly subjective indicators and do not indicate a level of mastery. They developed performance codes that consider a child's performance holistically and serve as a reflection of children's growth, not simply an average of progress from the beginning to the end of a grading period. (See "Performance Codes" below.) Heflebower, Hoegh, and Warrick (2014) emphasize that report cards should provide a "clear and meaningful" way to "report students' scores and growth over time" (66).

As Pappano (2010) recommends, the goal is to approach progress assessment in ways that encourage teachers to give children time to develop desired skills to full understanding. The team wanted to get away from simply measuring whether children have been trained to adequately perform a task. The new performance codes moved beyond that to reflect that idea and are further defined as follows:

Performance Level 1: The student does not have understanding of the entire concept/standard as expected for the grading period, even with support from the teacher.

Performance Codes	
4	Meets and applies expectations/standards independently
3	Meets and applies expectations/standards with support
2	Does not meet expectations/standards; may show growth with additional support
1	Does not meet expectations/standards; shows no growth even with support

Whole Child Indicators

Social and Emotional Development

> Works and plays with others

> Adapts to new situations

> Accepts responsibility

> Respects rights and property (personal and school)

> Solves problems

Learning Behaviors

> Demonstrates consistent effort

> Is attentive

> Follows rules and routines

Gross Motor Development and Ability

> Shows body/spatial/visual awareness

> Exhibits physical coordination and endurance

Fine Motor Development and Ability

> Uses school tools

> Takes care of personal needs

Communication Development and Ability

> Comprehends information through listening

> Demonstrates comprehension of information through speaking

Academic Indicators

Reading

> Concepts of print

> Phonological/phonemic awareness

> Phonics/word analysis

> Vocabulary

> Comprehension

Writing

> Conventions

> Purpose

Mathematics

> Number and operations

> Geometry

> Measurement

> Algebraic thinking

Performance Level 2: The student demonstrates inconsistent or partial understanding of the entire concept/standard as expected for the grading period, even with support from the teacher. The student may be marked below grade level and may not be on track for promotion.

Performance Level 3: The student has complete understanding of the entire concept/standard as expected for the grading period and is able to apply the knowledge consistently but with support from the teacher. The student is on grade level in an area in which he or she earns this code and on track for promotion.

Performance Level 4: The student has complete understanding of the entire concept/standard as expected for the grading period and is able to apply knowledge consistently and independently. The student is considered on or above grade level in an area in which he or she earns this code and on track for promotion.

It is important to note the difference between children demonstrating a skill independently and children needing support in order to demonstrate mastery. Children working independently are capable of thinking and acting on their own in individual, small group, or whole group situations. For children needing support, the teacher differentiates instruction and expectations for learning to enable them to understand and apply the standard independently. Further, some children may need step-by-step guidance or a higher degree of individualized feedback to demonstrate and apply the expectation or standard.

By completing the report card at the end of each school year quarter, kindergarten teachers can holistically evaluate children's development of cognitive, social, emotional, and physical skills. The school district uses the phrase *whole child indicators* to represent a continuum of developmental characteristics in the following areas:

> Social and emotional development

> Learning behaviors

> Gross motor development and ability

> Fine motor development and ability

> Communication development and ability

The expansion of the report card to include the whole child indicators follows a recommendation by Miller and Almon (2009) for creating effective and healthy kindergartens. They advise that "one-size-fits-all kindergarten standards" be replaced with "flexible guidelines based on well-grounded knowledge of children's cognitive, social, emotional, physical, and creative development" (6).

Children receive a performance code for each skill area listed in the Whole Child Indicators section. This section is strategically placed on the left side of the report card to emphasize to families the important role these characteristics play in child development and to increase the chance that families will read it before looking at the academic indicators section listed on the right side. (See sample indicators under "Whole Child Indicators" on page 94.)

The academic indicators, which are grouped under the content areas reading, writing, mathematics, science, and social studies, reflect the state kindergarten standards. Children receive a performance code (1, 2, 3, or 4) for each item. (See sample areas and indicators under "Academic Indicators" on page 94.)

Guides for Teachers and Families

In addition to the report card committee, a writing team made up of school district resources and kindergarten teachers wrote a guide for educators on using developmentally appropriate practices for kindergartners. The guide suggests practices that promote children's achievement in all areas and helps teachers to "weave district-mandated outcomes into lessons that teach but do not drill" (Wilson 2009, 2). Furthermore, the guide gives teachers the information necessary to accurately evaluate and consistently report children's progress. Each indicator on the report card gives teachers a comprehensive description, in the form of a rubric, for what a child's classroom performance will look like when the skill is fully mastered. This guide defines the indicators measured on the report card; it enables the school district to adjust to any changes in the kindergarten state learning standards without having to reformat the report card.

The same writing team developed a guide for families explaining the performance codes and report card indicators. This guide is distributed each time the report card is issued (four times per school year) and provides specific information on the standards assessed during that grading period. For example, the academic indicator Concepts of Print is defined in the first-quarter parent guide as "readily locates a word in print, knows the difference between letters and words, knows 15/26 upper- and 15/26 lowercase letters." Furthermore, the parent guide explains that level 4 is the desired outcome for the end of the kindergarten year, emphasizing the idea that children need time to fully develop skills in all areas. In addition, teachers are encouraged to review the progress report format and information with families before the first grading period each year.

Culturally and Linguistically Appropriate Assessment

A performance-based report card removes the idea that one size fits all and gives teachers flexibility in responding to children's individual needs. Whole child indicators provide a picture of children's social and emotional, learning, gross and fine motor, and communication skills and enable children, regardless of their background, to demonstrate their proficiency in a variety of ways. Narrow guidelines for reporting progress may not adequately measure children's learning and progress, but indicators such as "works and plays with others" and "adapts to new situations" are not restrictive. With the type of report card described in this article, teachers can more fully capture students' cultural and linguistic strengths as they assess children's individual development according to a set of standards rather than by mastery of discrete, isolated skills. It also gives teachers the flexibility to design learning activities that will reflect, develop, and complement students' unique backgrounds, knowledge, and skills.

The use of the revised report card is monitored through school visits and articulation with school administrators and classroom teachers. Teachers are required to carry out grading methodology in accordance with district procedures and provide families with progress reports in a format they can understand.

In 2013, a committee convened to begin developing a new report card for use in grades 1 through 6. This group determined that the new kindergarten progress report would be an appropriate model to use for developing the new report card for first and second grade students. The appeal of the new performance-based report card is that it is better aligned to the state standards and classroom teaching strategies.

Conclusion

Rather than providing a means to communicate progress, the school district's previous kindergarten report card was disconnected from the state learning standards and created additional work for teachers. School district staff, administrators, and teachers developed a new performance-based report card that met the child-progress reporting needs of educators and families. In addition, it reinforced a commitment to developmentally appropriate practices as essential to the kindergarten program.

During the first year of the new progress report's implementation, more than 80 percent of kindergarten families responding to an annual school district family survey rated it excellent or good. Although a formalized process outside family surveys has not been developed to evaluate the use of the new report card, consistent feedback from teachers indicates that the instrument is more effective in measuring and communicating children's outcomes than the previous one. The annual survey asks families to rate the information provided through the report card. In 2013, almost 96 percent of kindergarten parents rated the information provided through the progress report as excellent or good (1,395 responses). This data suggests overwhelming parental satisfaction with the new kindergarten report card. The authors believe this success is the result of a meaningful application of the NAEYC principles of developmentally appropriate practice in a manner that is beneficial for all stakeholders: children, their families, and their teachers.

Reflection Questions

1. What are the advantages of using a performance-based report card?

2. What are some ways you might use a performance-based report card to foster developmentally appropriate practices in your classroom?

3. Consider some of the ways your current reporting system affects how you teach. If it leads you to emphasize content areas at the expense of children's learning in other domains, what can you do to more holistically address their development?

4. How can a performance-based report card lead to improved communication with families about their children's progress?

5. If your school does not currently use a performance-based report card, how might you advocate for its adoption?

References

Goffin, S.G., & V. Washington. 2007. *Ready or Not: Leadership Choices in Early Care and Education.* Early Childhood Education series. New York: Teachers College Press.

Heflebower, T., J.K. Hoegh, & P. Warrick. With M. Hoback, M. McInteer, & B. Clemens. 2014. *A School Leader's Guide to Standards-Based Grading.* Bloomington, IN: Marzano Research.

Miller, E., & J. Almon. 2009. *Crisis in the Kindergarten: Why Children Need to Play in School.* College Park, MD: Alliance for Childhood. https://files.eric.ed.gov/fulltext/ED504839.pdf.

NAEYC. 2009. "Developmentally Appropriate Practice in Early Childhood Programs Serving Children from Birth Through Age 8." Position statement. Washington, DC: NAEYC. www.naeyc.org/sites/default/files /globally-shared/downloads/PDFs/resources/position-statements/PSDAP.pdf.

NAEYC & NAECS/SDE (National Association of Early Childhood Specialists in State Departments of Education). 2003. "Early Childhood Curriculum, Assessment, and Program Evaluation." Joint position statement. Washington, DC: NAEYC. www.naeyc.org/sites/default/files/globally-shared/downloads/PDFs /resources/position-statements/pscape.pdf.

NASDSE (National Association of State Directors of Special Education). 1994. "Summary of Goals 2000: Educate America Act." Alexandria, VA: NASDSE.

Pappano, L. 2010. "Kids Haven't Changed; Kindergarten Has: New Data Support a Return to 'Balance' in Kindergarten." *Harvard Education Letter* 26 (5). www.hepg.org/hel/article/479.

Wilson, D.M. 2009. "Developmentally Appropriate Practice in the Age of Testing: New Reports Outline Key Principles for PreK–3rd Grade." *Harvard Education Letter* 25 (3). www.hepg.org/hel/article/158.

About the Authors

Teresa Wright, EdD, is a director in the Brevard County (Florida) School Board Division of Leading and Learning. In addition to supervising elementary school principals, Dr. Wright administers the district Title I program, manages system accreditation, and secures additional funding through grant writing.

Barbara Murray, PhD, has served in education for more than 40 years as a public school teacher, middle school principal, high school principal, school district superintendent, and chair of the Brevard County School Board. She is an associate professor of educational leadership at the University of Central Florida, in Orlando, and has coauthored numerous books and journal articles.

Combating Assessment Fatigue in K–3 Classrooms

Vincent J. Costanza and Rick Falkenstein

No matter how dedicated or well trained, teachers cannot effect lasting, systemic change by themselves. Good teaching and good teachers need to be valued and supported by a rational system.

—Jacqueline Jones, *Early Literacy Assessment Systems: Essential Elements*

You have undoubtedly noticed that this is not a welcome time to talk about doing *more* assessment in early education. Teachers, parents, and students alike seem to feel that assessment has gotten in the way of teaching and learning. Assessment fatigue has set in among educators overwhelmed by the time and energy required to assess students and a corresponding lack of time for instruction. This feeling of fatigue is driven primarily by a lack of alignment between curriculum and assessment and a misunderstanding of the uses of assessment. Although we authors generally agree that too much assessment is occurring, we believe that a conversation on the purposes and types of assessment is needed before any understanding of an appropriate amount can be reached.

Particularly in early childhood, the fatigue is heightened by current assessment approaches, which are characterized by overassessment in particular areas and underassessment in others. There is a tremendous amount of assessment in the areas of literacy and math, for example, but limited attention to monitoring students' learning and growth in other areas, including social and emotional learning, approaches to learning, and science. This imbalance hampers an educator's ability to understand the full scope and developmental trajectories of children's learning. While many learning standards cover just two domains (i.e., literacy and math), the other areas have not lost relevance or importance for young children. Educators of young children ought to be given the time and resources to shape, monitor, and revise instruction across the full spectrum of development—and to assess learning in all areas as well. Recognition of the importance of educating the whole child has existed for a long time, and creating a rational system that aligns curriculum and assessment to meet the needs of the whole child is long overdue.

As educators and fathers of young children, the two of us understand and sympathize with the anxiety that permeates schools and households when discussing the role assessment has in understanding a child's development. While we want information that will help us assist our children in a wide range of areas—such as literacy, math, and approaches to learning—we, like many in the field, are concerned that the constant gathering of information gets in the way of teaching. To combat the fatigue the field faces, we must answer the following: How can educators guide their curricular and assessment decisions in a manner that balances the legitimate need to know how children are doing in areas such as literacy and math with understanding the full breadth of children's development?

This article provides some answers to this fundamental question, relevant to both teachers and administrators, by

> Defining *why* young children should be assessed in particular ways

> Connecting the *why* to *what* teachers should be doing with regard to assessment and *when* they should be doing it

> Describing effective *uses* of assessment data in K–3 settings

We'll then turn our attention to next steps and systems of support needed to help facilitate good teaching and create the rational system everyone desires.

Defining the Assessment *Why*

Assessing young children is not easy. Interacting with 5- to 8-year-olds who want your attention, miss a family member, need breakfast, or express excitement in the way only young children can is difficult. The challenging yet rewarding experience of teaching children is compounded by the need to understand whether they are learning what you are teaching them.

Moreover, knowing whether learning has occurred is not enough. Learning becomes more meaningful for instructional improvement as well as for communication with families when teachers can articulate *how* children are learning. While there are countless considerations to keep in mind when assessing young children, an important one is that children's learning is variable, uneven, idiosyncratic, and episodic (Shepard, Kagan, & Wurtz 1998). The learning a child displays on one day may not be displayed on another, or what appears solidly learned in one setting is not always applied to another. This is precisely why assessment methods that use multiple measures and sources of information over time give a clearer, more accurate picture of what a child knows and can do than an assessment that focuses on a single point in time.

What should be included on the canvas while attempting to paint a clear, accurate picture of a child's learning? Consider this thought experiment:

> Think about a child that you love. It could be your own child, a niece, a nephew, a grandchild, or a neighbor. Now, imagine you're attending back-to-school night for this child. As you sit in his or her classroom, the teacher asks you, "What do you want for your child this year?"

When we ask this question throughout the country, whether the audience is made up of state policy makers, district administrators, or second grade teachers, the following responses often come up:

I want my child to . . .

Be self-motivated

Love learning

Be happy

Help others

Be curious

If this is what we value for children, current instructional and assessment strategies are clearly missing valuable pieces of young children's learning. As architects of systems designed to improve the lives of children and families, it is worthwhile for educators to consider those pieces and ways to ensure that our systems of assessment account for the breadth of what the research has identified as—and what families and professionals believe are—significant in children's lives.

Many sources provide a description of the major developmental areas of young children. The National Research Council (NRC 2008) lists these five:

> Language and literacy development

> Cognition and general knowledge (including early math and scientific development)

> Approaches to learning (Hyson 2016)

> Physical well-being and motor development

> Social and emotional development

Recently, there has been much attention given to approaches to learning, which includes EPPIC skills—engagement, planning and problem solving, and initiative and creativity (Hyson 2016). There are clear connections between EPPIC skills and the skills educators aim to foster throughout a child's school experience as well as in life, yet the limited focus of assessment practices often forces educators into considering only language and literacy and cognition and general knowledge. As the adage goes, what gets measured gets done.

There is a wide range of reasons for assessing children, from evaluating a program to improving instructional practices for individuals and groups. The figure titled "Assessment Purpose-Type-Question (PTQ)" below demonstrates how each **purpose** of assessment should align with a particular **type** of assessment that is designed to answer a specific **question**. The PTQ chart is based in the foundations of the joint position statement from NAEYC and National Association of Early Childhood Specialists in State Departments of Education on curriculum, assessment, and program evaluation in early childhood (NAEYC & NAECS/SDE 2003).

While the relevant questions are not presented as an exhaustive list, the examples provided illustrate the connections to purpose, type, and question that should be considered. It is outside of the scope of this article to identify specific instruments that align to each purpose, but ensuring that your selected instrument aligns with the intended purpose of that instrument *and* allows you to answer a specific question is a good first step to take when clarifying your assessment landscape. If a single tool is being used to answer many questions or fulfill several purposes, an immediate red flag should be raised (Shepard, Kagan, & Wurtz 1998). Research-based assessment tools should be used only for their designed purpose.

Assessment Purpose-Type-Question (PTQ)

Assessment Purpose	Assessment Type	Assessment Question
To plan instruction for individual children and groups	Formative assessment	In what ways should instruction be modified?
To identify children in need of health or special services	Developmental screening	Is a child at risk for a potential learning delay?
To monitor trends and evaluate programs	Summative assessment	What is the efficacy of a curricular program?
To determine accountability of individual students, teachers, and the school	Summative assessment	Do children have better outcomes with teachers who have higher quality ratings?

How can you use the PTQ chart? Follow these three simple steps:

1. Work backwards: start by articulating the question you want to answer.
2. See if the type of assessment being considered will allow you to answer your question (e.g., a summative assessment will not give you actionable data to revise instruction because it is too far removed from teaching).
3. Determine whether the ultimate purpose is being addressed.

Connecting the *Why* to *What* and *When*

Clearly establishing which assessments you are using, why you are using them, and what information you'll gain from them will enable you to create a coherent assessment strategy—the key to successfully battling assessment fatigue. To help educators better coordinate their assessment efforts and ensure that their purpose coincides with a relevant assessment question, we walk them through an assessment mapping exercise that builds on the information shown in the PTQ chart. The figure titled "What, Why, and When of Assessment" below illustrates how a kindergarten teacher and a first grade teacher might strategize assessment throughout the school year to ensure that particular areas are covered but not overassessed.

Grade	What	Why	When
What, Why, and When of Assessment			
Kindergarten	Developmental Screening	**Purpose:** To identify children in need of health or special services **Question:** Is a child at risk for a potential learning delay?	Upon entry into the program and completed by no later than the end of October* *For children who were not screened in preschool
	Formative/ Observational/ Curriculum-Embedded Assessment	**Purpose:** To plan instruction for individual children and groups **Question:** In what ways should instruction be modified?	Ongoing with three to five rating periods
	Formative/ Criterion-Referenced Assessment of Literacy	**Purpose:** To monitor the progress of reading skills **Question:** In what ways should literacy instruction be modified?	January and June
First	Formative/ Criterion-Referenced Assessment of Literacy	**Purpose:** To monitor the progress of reading skills **Question:** In what ways should literacy instruction be modified?	October, January, and June
	Formative/ Observational Assessment	**Purpose:** To plan instruction for individual children and groups **Question:** In what ways should instruction be modified?	Ongoing with three to five rating periods
	Summative Assessment	**Purpose:** To examine strengths and needs, both in the classroom and throughout the school **Question:** What is the efficacy of a curricular program?	May

To use this mapping exercise,

1. Start with the purpose of assessment in the *why* column. Complete the *why* column by identifying the questions you want to answer.

2. Fill in the *what* column, adding specific instruments that align to the designated purpose.

3. Use the *when* column to plan ahead and ensure that your various assessment efforts don't overlap unnecessarily and overburden you.

Going through the mapping exercise also prompts educators to reflect on important considerations, such as

> Are teachers overburdened at certain times of the year?

> Are developmental areas missing?

> Are we overassessing in some areas and underassessing in others?

This process also includes an implicit fourth step that centers on considerations for data use, discussed in the next section.

Effective Uses of Assessment Data in K–3 Settings

One strategy that will assist with the use of assessment data in kindergarten through third grade settings is a systematic focus on instruction that defines best practices and directly connects them to the work of teachers and administrators. Assessment in the early years should be closely tied to the curriculum as well as the developmental areas described earlier.

Initiatives that aim to align teachers', administrators', and families' understanding of best practices in the early years are well positioned to combat assessment fatigue. For instance, the initiative behind the development of *First Through Third Grade Implementation Guidelines* sought to define best practices in the primary years and assisted with the application of academically rigorous and developmentally appropriate curricular and assessment practices (NJDOE 2015; Riley-Ayers et al. 2017). Simply put, the conversations about assessment and curriculum are inextricably linked. Assessing in particular ways requires curricular approaches that accommodate embedded assessment.

While defining best practices is a significant first step in the alignment of quality curriculum and assessment, documents alone will not change practice. To inform and shape practice, targeted professional development is needed, with three key elements that contribute to effective implementation of best practices and curricular and assessment cohesion. Professional development should

> **Be ongoing throughout the year.** Focus on teacher-led problems of practice that are relevant to the daily lives of teachers, such as room arrangement, scheduling, standards alignment, and monitoring growth over time.

> **Involve both teachers and administrators.** Focus on best practices and information tailored to teachers and administrators; each group's roles impact the other's as well as the implementation of best practices. For example, building schedules will impact the implementation of classroom schedules.

> **Employ a variety of methods.** Include best practice videos, expert instructors, and Professional Learning Communities (PLCs) that are coordinated at the building and district levels to provide the relevant supports to implement newly learned practices.

Together, these elements of professional development help to create the opportunities and space needed to have conversations around the best ways to assess children's learning using all of the elements in the assessment map.

Next Steps

There are two clear action steps for addressing assessment fatigue. The first is a call to action in the field to update assessment research and practices. More research is needed on how the data gleaned from specific instruments fits together and assists educators in understanding how children are doing throughout the early learning continuum. For example, in first grade, it is important to know about reading development, but how does an understanding about reading levels inform a summative assessment about comprehension, math, science, or social and emotional development? For years, educators have been forced to emphasize some of these content areas over others, and without research to inform how these assessments fit together, the fatigue will continue.

Since this call to action will not happen overnight, the second step is a more immediate strategy for districts and school systems to build habits to change the culture around assessment: creating a frame for curricular and assessment cohesion. We encourage districts to follow the four steps outlined by Michael Fullan and Joanne Quinn (2015):

1. Capacity building: focused direction to build collective purpose

2. Collaborative: cultivating collaborative cultures while clarifying individual and team roles

3. Pedagogy: deepening learning to accelerate improvement and foster innovation

4. Systemness: securing accountability from the inside out (5)

What are the immediate actions a district could take to build the habits that change the culture around assessment? Build capacity by focusing on teacher *and* administrator understanding. Collaborate to build partnerships with state agencies as well as other

Reflection Questions

1. Do the teachers and administrators in your school or district have a common understanding of research-based assessment and curricular practices for kindergarten through third grade? What could be done to find additional common ground?

2. Select an assessment instrument you use in your classroom. Using the PTQ chart, analyze how well it aligns with that instrument's intended purpose and whether it provides information to help you answer a specific question. If it does not accomplish these things, consider meeting with teachers and administrators to research tools that align to the purpose.

3. Consider how your school's or district's assessment practices currently connect with its curricular practices. If there is a disconnect, identify areas that lead to the disconnect and consider the teaching practices you want to promote and the ways you would like children to display understanding.

4. What opportunities do the teachers and administrators in your school or district have to regularly discuss questions about assessing young children? How could additional opportunities be created?

districts facing similar problems of practice. Place pedagogy on a pedestal by focusing on instruction in all activities, including PLCs. Take a system approach that links assessment initiatives to curricular initiatives, and "never send a changed individual into an unchanged culture" (Fullan 2003, 4).

Conclusion

The assessment conversation cannot happen in isolation of other educational conversations occurring in a building, district, and beyond. "Without accompanying changes in the way that work gets done, only the potential for improvement exists" (Garvin 1993).

These words, which are important when describing the development of a learning organization, must be applied to the adults in the schooling organization. As educators, we often speak of teaching children how to learn. It would appear that when it comes to assessing their learning, we need to do some more learning ourselves. Until our learning is linked to some changed behaviors that foster curricular and assessment coherence, the assessment landscape will not look rational to teachers and certainly not to children. The fatigue of assessment is not preordained; it is time to turn that fatigue into an energy that moves each of us to be wide awake to the possibilities for, and development of, all children in our care.

References

Fullan, M. 2003. "Implementing Change at the Building Level." In *Best Practices, Best Thinking, and Emerging Issues in School Leadership*, eds. W. Owings & L. Kaplan, 31–36. Thousand Oaks, CA: Corwin.

Fullan, M., & J. Quinn. 2015. *Coherence: The Right Drivers in Action for Schools, Districts, and Systems*. Thousand Oaks, CA: Corwin.

Garvin, D.A. 1993. "Building a Learning Organization." *Harvard Business Review* 71 (4): 78–91. https://hbr
.org/1993/07/building-a-learning-organization.

Hyson, M. 2016. *Approaches to Learning: Kindergarten to Grade 3 Guide.* Trenton, NJ: New Jersey
Department of Education. www.state.nj.us/education/ece/rttt/k3/guide.pdf.

NAEYC & NAECS/SDE (National Association of Early Childhood Specialists in State Departments of
Education). 2003. "Early Childhood Curriculum, Assessment, and Program Evaluation." Joint position
statement. Washington, DC: NAEYC. www.naeyc.org/sites/default/files/globally-shared/downloads/PDFs
/resources/position-statements/pscape.pdf.

NJDOE (New Jersey Department of Education). 2015. *First Through Third Grade Implementation
Guidelines.* Trenton, NJ: NJDOE. www.state.nj.us/education/ece/rttt/ImplementationGuidelines1-3.pdf.

NRC (National Research Council). 2008. *Early Childhood Assessment: Why, What, and How.* Washington,
DC: National Academies Press. doi:10.17226/12446.

Riley-Ayers, S., S. Ryan, A. Figueras-Daniel, & V.J. Costanza. 2017. "Giving Young Students a Bigger Slice of
the Pie (Chart)." *Preschool Matters Today* (blog). March 17. http://nieer.org/2017/03/17/giving-young
-students-bigger-slice-pie-chart.

Shepard, L., S.L. Kagan, & E. Wurtz, eds. 1998. *Principles and Recommendations for Early Childhood
Assessments.* Washington, DC: National Education Goals Panel. http://govinfo.library.unt.edu/negp
/reports/prinrec.pdf.

About the Authors

Vincent J. Costanza, EdD, oversees all educational content and research initiatives as chief academic officer at Teaching Strategies. Previously he led the Division of Early Childhood Education & Family Engagement at the New Jersey Department of Education. He currently serves on the boards of NAEYC and the New Jersey affiliate of ASCD (NJASCD) and has served as vice president of the National Association of Early Childhood Specialists in State Departments of Education (NAECS/SDE) and as an elected school board member.

Rick Falkenstein is superintendent of Kingwood Township School District in New Jersey, where he has been a teacher, principal, and superintendent for almost 20 years. He regularly conducts workshops on the importance of high-quality early childhood programs. Through his partnership with New Jersey's Division of Early Childhood, the district was the first in the state to implement a program for preschool through second grade that focuses on children's academic, social, and emotional development.

Photographs: pp. 98, 103, © Getty Images

Spotlight books created just for you!

Covering a broad range of subjects, this bestselling series includes articles carefully curated from NAEYC's award-winning *Young Children* journal.

Each book includes research-based articles and questions to help readers reflect on the content of the articles and on their practice. Perfect for higher education courses and in-service workshops!

Spotlight on Young Children: Social and Emotional Development

Item 2850
2017 • 116 pages

Spotlight on Young Children: Teaching and Learning in the Primary Grades

Item 2841
2016 • 136 pages

Spotlight on Young Children: Exploring Play

Item 2840
2015 • 136 pages

Spotlight on Young Children: Supporting Dual Language Learners

Item 2210
2014 • 104 pages

Spotlight on Young Children: Exploring Language and Literacy

Item 2830
2014 • 112 pages

Spotlight on Young Children: Exploring Science

Item 373
2013 • 80 pages

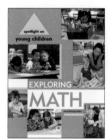

Spotlight on Young Children: Exploring Math

Item 367
2012 • 64 pages

Spotlight on Young Children and Technology

Item 267
2012 • 72 pages

Spotlight on Young Children and Families

Item 288
2007 • 64 pages